Sexual

Harassment

Investigations

SEXUAL HARASSMENT INVESTIGATIONS

HOW TO LIMIT YOUR LIABILITY AND MORE

A PRACTICAL GUIDE

ARJUN P. AGGARWAL
M.A., LL.M., J.S.D.

and

MADHU M. GUPTA
B.Sc., LL.B., J.D.

HARASSMENT PUBLICATIONS
Ottawa, Canada

Sexual Harassment Investigations:
How to Limit Your Liability and More - A Practical Guide

National Library of Canada Cataloguing in Publication

Aggarwal, Arjun P. (Arjun Prakash), 1929 -
Sexual harassment investigations: how to limit your liability and more: a practical
      guide / by Arjun P. Aggarwal and Madhu M. Gupta.

ISBN 0-9735335-0-1

    1. Sexual harassment—Investigation. I. Gupta, Madhu M., 1967-
II. Title.

HF5549.5.S45A38   2004   658.3'145   C2004-902479-5

Printed and bound in Canada.

Harassment Publications

Canada:	U.S.A.:
54 Fieldcrest Avenue	4715 Chokeberry Drive
Ottawa, Ontario	Naperville, IL
K2J 4Y8	60654
Phone: (613) 823-8743	Phone: (630) 922-5623

Email: harassment_publications@yahoo.ca

About the Authors

Dr. Arjun P. Aggarwal, M.A., LL.M, J.S.D., is an Ottawa-based expert on workplace harassment issues. He is a Human Rights Consultant, Labour Arbitrator, and former Professor of Human Rights and Industrial Relations. He was also a member of the Canadian Human Rights Tribunal, a member of the Board of Inquiry under the Ontario Human Rights Act, a member of the Council of the College of Physicians and Surgeons of Ontario and a vice-chair for the Ontario Workers' Compensation Appeals Tribunal.

Dr. Aggarwal is the author of the leading study, *Sexual Harassment in the Workplace* (Butterworths 3rd ed. 2000), *Sexual Harassment – A Guide for Understanding and Prevention* (Butterworths 1992), *Sex Discrimination: Employment Law and Practices* (Butterworths 1994), and *Sexual Harassment on Campus: A Guide for Students and Teachers* (M. M. Publications 1985). He has also published a number of law journal articles. His writings and talks on human rights and harassment have also been translated and published in Japanese law journals.

Dr. Aggarwal is widely acknowledged as Canada's leading authority on sexual harassment. His work has frequently been quoted by the courts, human rights tribunals and arbitrators, and his text has also been cited by the Supreme Court of Canada.

Madhu M. Gupta resides in Chicago, Illinois, where she practiced with the law firm of Chapman and Cutler. She earned her J.D. from the University of Michigan Law School where she was awarded the Order of the Coif, and she received her LL.B. from the University of Calgary. She is a member of the State Bars of Illinois and of the District of Columbia. She is also co-author of *Sexual Harassment in the Workplace*, and *Same-Sex Sexual Harassment: Is it Sex Discrimination? A Review of Canadian and American Law.*

DEDICATION

*To all those who are committed to
providing a discrimination and
harassment free work environment*

ACKNOWLEDGEMENT

I am grateful to many of my friends and colleagues from across the country who have provided me with challenging insight and thought-provoking stimulation which forced me to objectively and thoroughly examine the issues of investigation.

I am particularly indebted to Aaron Berg, General Counsel of the Manitoba Human Rights Commission for his guidance, encouragement, and assistance throughout the preparation of this book.

Special thanks are due to: Charles Ferris, Special Counsel of the New Brunswick Human Rights Commission; Andrew Pinto from the law firm of Eberts Symes Street Pinto & Jull; Rabindra Kanungo, Professor Emeritus, Faculty of Management, McGill University; Bryan Luce, Vice President, Human Resources, Manitoba Telecom Services Inc.; Gerald Foley, Director, Employee Relations, B.C. Ferry Services Inc.; Rod LeDuc, Manager, Human Resources, Gerdau Ameristeel; Shirley Voyna Wilson, Sexual Harassment Advisor, University of Calgary; and Mary Anne McNeill, formerly of Butterworths Canada for generously reviewing the manuscript and making invaluable suggestions.

I am also grateful to Mike Glynn, Registrar, Greg Miller, Legal Counsel, and the members and staff of the Canadian Human Rights Tribunal; Helen Beck, Counsel, Justice Canada, Human Resources Development Canada; and Diane Roller, Sexual Harassment Officer, University of Ottawa, for their encouragement and support. Thanks are also due to Suzanne Tourigny, Chief Librarian of the Canadian Human Rights Commission for assisting with research material.

Finally, I would like to pay tribute to my wife, Mithilesh, for her unwavering support, hard work, encouragement and patience, without which this book would not have been possible.

Arjun P. Aggarwal
Ottawa, Ontario
July 2004

TABLE OF CONTENTS

xv

S exual harassment is all too common an occurrence in the workplace, so much so that we read and hear about it regularly on the news. Now more than ever, employers have an obligation to protect their employees from sexual harassment and to provide them with a harassment free work environment. A harassment free workplace simply means that all employees are treated equally and fairly, with respect and dignity, irrespective of creed, sex, age, sexual orientation, race, religion, or disability, etc. No one, including supervisors and managers should be allowed to abuse their authority and power.

A harassment free work environment is not a luxury but an economic, social, legal and political necessity. It is essential for maintaining a contented, productive and motivated workforce. Employees must not only be treated with respect and dignity, they must also *feel* that they are being treated as such. Women in non-traditional jobs, new immigrants, visible minorities and aboriginal people are particular targets of hostility and harassment. See for example the *Commodore* case.[1]

Harassers, regardless of how high an office they may hold, are polluters of the work environment. If an organization does not take the necessary steps to rectify the work environment as soon as harassment is noticed, it may end up paying a higher price later in the form of a dissatisfied workforce, low morale, loss in productivity, ongoing litigation, bad publicity and damage to its reputation. Clearly, the costs of immediately addressing harassment situations are much lower than allowing unacceptable behaviour to continue unchecked.

Once sexual harassment has occurred in the workplace, it must be investigated properly. In order to effectively investigate sexual harassment one needs to ask questions such as the following: What role does an investigator play in addressing sexual harassment? How can an effective investigation be conducted? How can employers discharge their obligations? How can they limit or eliminate their liability? What are the preventive and remedial steps that an employer needs to take? How can a sexual harassment policy combat harassment?

Human rights tribunals and courts have explicitly stated the obligations and liabilities of employers. What are needed now are the requisite tools to conduct effective investigations into allegations of harassment and to combat and eliminate it.

Justice Sopinka of the Supreme Court of Canada has pointed out that investigators, the human rights commissions, and reviewing courts are essentially without legislative guidance regarding the conduct of investigations.[2] Legislatures, tribunals, commissions and the courts – none has provided any clear, concise, systematic analysis of the required elements of an investigation in a human rights complaint. That said, the courts and tribunals have often criticized the manner in which investigations have been conducted, both by employers and by commissions. Their thoughts with respect to how a proper investigation should be conducted have been disseminated through judicial pronouncements. We have worked backwards to piece together the elements required for a good investigation, by analyzing what has been determined to be a faulty investigation and what has failed to meet the standards and requirements of the law.

We have reflected on the learned thoughts and commentaries in the wide variety of case law and utilized the knowledge and experience from Canadian and American harassment investigators to compile these ideas together in a systematic and organized manner to provide a guide for an effective investigation. After examining the merits and demerits of the investigations conducted by the commissions and employers, we have arranged the information in a format which corresponds to the judicial standards and which will hopefully be of assistance to investigators and litigators alike. The text has been divided into five parts:

Part One overviews the law on sexual harassment, answering questions such as What is sexual harassment? and What behaviour amounts to sexual harassment? It explains the difference between – "Quid Pro Quo" and "Offensive Work Environment" harassment. It also examines the employer's responsibility and liability for harassment by its supervisors, employees, and non-employees. Part One highlights how costly workplace harassment could be for employers, and what affirmative steps employers should take to stop harassment.

Part Two deals with preventive measures, outlining the steps that employers should and *should not* take to prevent harassment or minimize its effects if harassment has occurred. It studies the important role supervisors play in preventing harassment at the initial stages. Key ingredients for an effective sexual harassment policy and complaint resolution procedure are outlined. Finally, Part Two examines the thorny issues surrounding workplace romances and harassment complaints against senior management.

Part Three describes the corrective and remedial steps that employers should take to resolve harassment complaints. It discusses the role of mediation and how early mediation can be effective and satisfying to resolve complaints. The basic requirements for an effective, prompt, fair, thorough and unbiased investigation are examined.

Part Four provides various investigation models the employer can choose depending on the type of workplace and the nature and severity of the allegations. It includes criteria for selecting the right

20

investigator, and it discusses the advantages of having joint union-management investigations.

Part Five is the most significant part of the book. It provides step-by-step procedures for the investigator to follow including: planning for an investigation, conducting interviews, determining credibility, maintaining an accurate record, and drafting the investigation report for management. Emphasis is given to interviewing and investigation techniques. Part Five concludes by outlining the penalties and the redress mechanisms available.

The difference between a good and a poor investigation can determine whether an employer will be held accountable for the sexual harassment. The importance of conducting prompt, fair and effective internal investigations is further highlighted by the Canadian Human Rights Act Review Panel ("LaForest Panel"). The LaForest Panel recommends that where the employer can demonstrate that it has an effective internal responsibility system in place for resolving claims, the tribunal should have the power to dismiss a claim unless the internal system failed to fully deal with the human rights issues or failed to provide an adequate remedy. The LaForest Panel indirectly raises the employer's internal process to a quasi-judical level.

We have ventured in this book to deal with these issues and to provide some helpful tools for conducting a successful investigation. We hope this book will prove equally useful to the readers as our text *Sexual Harassment in the Workplace* has been over the years.

Finally, while we have focused specifically on the issue of sexual harassment, the principles and guidelines for conducting a successful and legally sound investigation presented in this book are transferable to investigating complaints based on other prohibited grounds of discrimination, such as race, religion and national or ethnic origin.

PART I

HARASSMENT LAW THAT

INVESTIGATORS NEED TO KNOW

HARASSMENT LAW THAT INVESTIGATORS NEED TO KNOW*

Sexual harassment is illegal and it is prohibited by human rights statutes. Generally, sexual harassment is a civil wrong; however, if the harassing behaviour extends to sexual assault it also becomes a criminal offence.

Sexual harassment law has developed and broadened significantly since 1980, when an Ontario Board of Inquiry, in the first Canadian sexual harassment case, *Bell v. Ladas,*[3] discussed at some length whether or not sexual harassment constituted discrimination on the basis of sex. This case laid down the foundation of sexual harassment law in Canada by declaring that "sexual harassment amounts to sex discrimination prohibited under the *Ontario Human Rights Code.*"[4]

Other Canadian jurisdictions followed the philosophy and reasoning of *Bell v. Ladas* and held that sexual harassment amounted to discrimination on the basis of sex and was prohibited under their relevant human rights statutes. Finally, in 1989, in *Janzen v. Platy Enterprises Ltd.,*[5] the Supreme Court of Canada confirmed that sexual harassment was a form of sex discrimination and that it was unwelcome conduct of a sexual nature that detrimentally affected the work environment or led to adverse job-related consequences for the victim.

---

* Part I is partially based on the authors' earlier text *Sexual Harassment in the Workplace*, (Butterworths 3rd ed. 2000) and is reproduced with permission of LexisNexis Canada Inc. Copyright 2000.

CHAPTER 1

A. What is Sexual Harassment?

S exual harassment is not easy to define. Whenever groups of individuals are together, sexual attraction between individuals and the possible evolution of this attraction into relationships is inevitable. What makes sexual harassment different from flirting or casual social asides is that it is unwanted by the recipient.

Sexual harassment is any unwelcome attention of a sexual nature that occurs while working or seeking employment that jeopardizes a person's ability to earn a living. As stated earlier, sexual harassment is a form of discrimination based on sex.

A formal definition of sexual harassment has been provided by the Equal Employment Opportunity Commission in the United States (EEOC): Unwelcome sexual advances, requests for sexual favours, and other verbal or physical conduct of a sexual nature constitutes sexual harassment when:

      1. submission to such conduct is made either explicitly or

implicitly a term or condition of an individual's employment,

2. submission to or rejection of such conduct by an individual is used as the basis for employment decisions affecting such individual; or

3. such conduct has the purpose or effect of unreasonably interfering with an individual's work performance or creating an intimidating, hostile, or offensive working environment.

Chief Justice Dickson of the Supreme Court of Canada in *Janzen v. Platy Enterprises Ltd.*[6] described sexual harassment in the following words:

> I am of the view that sexual harassment in the workplace may be broadly defined as unwelcome conduct of a sexual nature that detrimentally affects the work environment or leads to adverse job related consequences for the victims of the harassment. It is . . . an *abuse of power*. When sexual harassment occurs in the workplace, it is an abuse of both economic and sexual power. Sexual harassment is a demeaning practice, one that constitutes a profound affront to the dignity of the employees forced to endure it. *By requiring an employee to contend with unwelcome sexual actions or explicit sexual demands, sexual harassment in the workplace attacks the dignity and self-respect of the victim both as an employee and as a human being.* [Emphasis added.]

Therefore, we can say that sexual harassment is behaviour that is both sexual in nature and is unwanted by the person towards whom it is directed. To constitute harassment, the behaviour must generally affect the recipient's employment, instruction or participation in educational activities, or interfere with the recipient's work environment, performance, or evaluation.

In determining whether the alleged conduct constitutes sexual harassment, consideration is given to the totality of the circumstances, including the nature of the sexual advance and the context in which the alleged incident(s) occurred.

B. What Behaviour Constitutes Sexual Harassment?

There is a wide divergence of perceptions in our society as to what words or actions constitute sexual harassment. The complexity of human behaviour makes it difficult to pinpoint exactly what behaviour a particular individual will perceive as harassment. Sexist attitudes and behaviour are highly persistent in our society, and it is often difficult to draw the line between what is **acceptable behaviour** and what is **unacceptable behaviour** in the workplace. To one person, placing an arm around the shoulder of another may be perceived as a gesture of support; to another, the same gesture may be offensive and harassing.

Sexual behaviour that a person finds personally offensive *may* be considered sexual harassment. Such behaviour may be subtle or obvious, verbal or non-verbal.

<u>FORMS</u>
<u>OF SEXUAL HARASSMENT</u>:

VERBAL BEHAVIOUR
NON-VERBAL BEHAVIOUR (GESTURE)
VISUAL ACTIVITY
PHYSICAL CONTACT
PSYCHOLOGICAL BEHAVIOUR

Sexually harassing behaviour covers a wide range of conduct that runs the gamut including:

- patting or pinching an individual's bottom as he/she walks

down the hall;
- hugging, kissing or blowing kisses;
- repeated, intrusive, insistent arms around the shoulder;
- repeated unwanted social invitations;
- gestures such as leering and ogling with suggestive overtones;
- lewd gestures such as hand or sign language to denote sexual activity;
- sexual jokes or jokes about gender specific traits;
- an atmosphere contaminated with degrading comments or innuendoes, and/or references to one's sex life;
- remarks about a woman's or man's body;
- displays of derogatory images of men/women or pornography;
- the requirement that employees wear revealing uniforms that leave them the target of sexual comments and propositions from the general public;
- explicit propositions to engage in sexual relations or be terminated (or suffer some other adverse job-related consequences); and
- sexual assault.

C. Types of Sexual Harassment

There are two basic forms of sexual harassment:
1. "Quid Pro Quo" – Giving one valuable thing for another; and
2. Poisonous or Offensive Work Environment.

1. Quid Pro Quo

Quid pro quo sexual harassment occurs when someone with authority behaves in a sexually harassing manner towards another individual with less power dangling negative job-related consequences as blackmail. Continued employment, advancement or other job benefits become explicitly or implicitly conditioned upon the acquiescence to the sexual demands of the harasser.

In such situations, the employee is forced to decide between submitting to sexual demands and forfeiting some employment benefits. Adverse job-related consequences may vary in form and degree of severity from employee to employee in different circumstances. Consequences may range from assigning unpleasant tasks, reduction in hours, transfer, demotion, denial of promotion, or denial of permanent status, to dismissal or threat of dismissal. Dismissal is the equivalent of capital punishment in an employer/employee relationship.

The *quid pro quo* concept is also known as "the tangible benefits theory," under which negative employment repercussions must be shown to have resulted directly from a refusal of the harasser's sexual demands. *Olarte v. Commodore Business Machines*,[7] provides a typical example of adverse job-related consequences for resisting the sexual advances of a supervisor. In *Olarte*, the Board of Inquiry found that the respondent engaged in a practice of sexual harassment against the complainants. In his position as foreman, the respondent repeatedly touched and kissed the complainants, asked them for invitations to their homes, and requested that they engage in sexual intercourse with him. When his advances were refused, the respondent penalized the complainants by shouting at them, finding fault with their work, and shifting them to heavier duties, with the result that some of the complainants quit and one was fired.

2. Poisonous or Offensive Work Environment

Sexual harassment in the workplace frequently creates a hostile, intimidating and discriminating environment. Courts and tribunals have used various terms including "atmosphere of discrimination" and "sexually derogatory work environment" to describe a workplace that is poisoned by sexual harassment.

Under this type of harassment, submission to the sexually harassing conduct is not necessarily or explicitly made a term of employment; nevertheless, the individual is forced to work in an environment which is intimidating, hostile and offensive. The work environment becomes unpleasant or unbearable to the victim because of a pattern of comments, insults and hostility. A poisoned work environment may result from the rejection of a sexual proposition or advance or it may exist even without such overt action by any particular supervisor or co-worker.

Though an employee suffers no loss of benefits or tenure, the employee's psychological health may be harmed and she/he may feel uncomfortable in the workplace. The creation of an offensive or hostile work environment by itself, constitutes a violation of the human rights statutes. Consequently, an employee subjected to such an environment need not prove additional tangible detriment.

3. Determine Whether the Work Environment is Hostile

Establishing that sexual harassment has created a hostile work environment is not easy or straightforward. Some courts and tribunals have stated that the harassment must be sufficiently severe or pervasive to alter the conditions of employment and create an abusive and poisonous working environment.

To determine if an environment is hostile, the following factors are generally taken into consideration:

- Whether the conduct was verbal, physical, or both;
- How frequently it was repeated;
- Whether the conduct was hostile and patently offensive;
- Whether the alleged harasser was a co-worker or supervisor;
- Whether other employees joined in perpetrating the harassment;
- Whether the harassment was directed at more than one individual; and
- Whether the conduct stopped after warning.

When evaluating these factors, the main question is whether the conduct unreasonably interfered with the complainant's work performance or created an intimidating, hostile or offensive work environment.

In cases where the alleged sexual harassment consisted solely of verbal conduct, gestures or visual conduct, the following inquiries are normally made:

- Did the alleged harasser single out the complainant?
- Did the complainant voluntarily participate in sexual humour or jokes, or other sexual behaviour?
- What was the relationship between the complainant and the alleged harasser?
- Were the remarks, gestures or visual conduct offensive or derogatory?

A hostile or poisonous work environment claim is actionable as sexual harassment under human rights law. The employer is liable if he/she knew or should have known of the sexual harassment. If actual or constructive knowledge exists and if the employer failed to take immediate and appropriate corrective action, the employer would be held directly liable.

Usually an employer acquires actual knowledge by firsthand observation, by an internal complaint to a supervisor or manager, or by a formal complaint of discrimination or harassment. An employer is liable when it knew or upon reasonably diligent inquiry should have known of the harassment. If the sexual harassment is shown to be pervasive, it may give rise to an inference of knowledge or establish constructive knowledge.

We can draw some further general guidelines for what behaviour would constitute a hostile environment:

- The more outrageous the behaviour, the more likely that the behaviour will be found to constitute sexual harassment. Also, the more offensive the behaviour, the more likely that one single incident alone will be enough to constitute sexual harassment.
- Behaviour is more likely to be viewed as unwelcome if the individual objects to the conduct the very first time. However, even if the individual has previously condoned the conduct, once he/she informs the harasser that the behaviour is unwelcome, previous tolerance of the conduct

is negated.

Chief Justice Dickson, writing for the Supreme Court of Canada in *Janzen v. Platy Enterprises Ltd.*[8], downplayed the distinction made by some Canadian courts and human rights tribunals between *"quid pro quo"* and "hostile environment" sexual harassment. He stated:

> Canadian human rights tribunals have also tended to rely on the *quid pro quo*/hostile work environment dichotomy. *I do not find this categorization particularly helpful. While the distinction may have been important to illustrate forcefully the range of behaviour that constitutes harassment at a time before sexual harassment was widely viewed as actionable, in my view there is no longer any need to characterize harassment as one of these forms.*

D. Same-Sex Sexual Harassment

Same-sex sexual harassment is not uncommon in Canada, particularly in male-dominated areas such as in the military and sports industry.[9] However, same-sex sexual harassment victims may be *even more* reluctant to report harassment for fear of the stigmatism of homosexuality associated with same-sex sexual harassment. *Same*-sex sexual harassment may be found in any of the following forms:

1. Sexual harassment by a heterosexual male towards a male or heterosexual female towards a female,
2. Sexual harassment by a homosexual male towards a male or by a homosexual female towards a female, or
3. Sexual harassment by a bisexual person towards a male or a female of the same gender.

Romman v. Sea-West Holdings Ltd.[10] was the first Canadian case where a male employee alleged that his male supervisor sexually harassed him. The complainant alleged that the skipper of a tug sexually harassed him by grabbing his genitals and patting him in the genital area.

When he complained about these sexual advances to the owner, his services were terminated. The Canadian Human Rights Tribunal found that the company was guilty of sexual harassment and observed:

> It should never be part of a person's employment environment, or part of their employment situation, to have to submit to the touching of the genitals. That must be seen as unacceptable. Nobody should have to put up with that as part of having a job.

In *Cassidy v. Sanchez*[11] the complainant, a male employee, alleged that his male supervisor, Mr. Sanchez, sexually harassed him during his employment. Cassidy alleged that when he resisted Sanchez's sexual invitations and advances, his employment was terminated. The offending sexual conduct included patting his buttocks, touching his crotch, and inviting him home to share liquor and drugs. When Cassidy asked to be paid, Sanchez put his arm around him and said that he "could get paid any time he wanted." The British Columbia Human Rights Tribunal held that Sanchez's actions towards Cassidy constituted sexual harassment.

In *Van Berkel v. MPI Security Ltd.*[12] a 19-year-old female employee, Van Berkel, was sexually harassed by a female co-owner of the business, Mrs. Banks. Van Berkel alleged that Banks made several comments about her appearance and clothing. According to Van Berkel, Banks said that Van Berkel had a "hot little body;" Banks said she could see Van Berkel's underwear through a white skirt she wore one day; she touched Van Berkel on the buttocks in a sexual way several times; and she told Van Berkel that she "would probably look great naked." Van Berkel resigned because of the sexual harassment and filed a complaint with the B.C. Human Rights Commission.

The basic issue before the B.C. Human Rights Tribunal was whether sexual harassment by a person of the same sex constituted discrimination within the meaning of the *B.C. Human Rights Act*. The tribunal found in favour of Van Berkel, and held that Banks sexually harassed her.

The case of *Hanes v. M&M Ventures and Wight*[13] dealt with sexual harassment involving two heterosexual women. The workplace was a truck stop staffed entirely by women. The complainant, a female employee, alleged that her female supervisor sexually harassed her by touching her genitals. The complainant had recently separated from her husband and felt that her marital situation was used as an excuse by other employees to comment on her sex life. She alleged that co-workers joked about setting her up with various men for dates and/or sexual encounters.

The Saskatchewan Board of Inquiry, after reviewing various definitions of sexual harassment, which generally involved the power dynamic between men and women, concluded that the prohibition on sexual harassment was not confined to male against female harassment. The Board expressly recognized that same-sex sexual harassment constituted sex discrimination prohibited under Canadian law. The Board held that it should never be part of an employee's employment environment, or part of their employment situation, to have to submit to the touching of the genitals. The Board held that such behaviour was an affront to the complainant's sexual dignity as a woman, and thus constituted sexual harassment.

It is obvious from a review of the Canadian same-sex cases that there is little controversy in the Canadian legal profession over whether same-sex sexual harassment is sexual harassment. The issue of the harasser's gender and/or sexual orientation was not raised nor discussed in these cases. So long as the conduct of the harasser was sexual in nature, offensive and unwanted, such conduct amounted to sexual harassment. Same-sex sexual harassment is simply to be afforded the same treatment as opposite-sex sexual harassment.

Same-sex harassment, so far, has not been a large issue in the Canadian context. But this issue seems to be on the horizon. A U.S. study shows that same-sex sexual harassment has increased approximately 6% from the year 2000 to the year 2002. Although the Canadian tribunals have not distinguished between heterosexual and same-sex harassment, as a precaution, employers should specifically prohibit same-sex harassment as well as harassment of homosexuals in their anti-harassment policy.

E. Transgender Harassment

The expression "transgender" is often also referred to as "transsexual." According to the *Oxford Dictionary*, a "transsexual is a person born with the physical characteristics of one sex who emotionally and psychological feels that he belongs to the opposite sex." *The American Heritage Dictionary* describes, a "transsexual is a person with an overwhelming desire to become the other sex or a person whose sex has been changed externally through surgery."

Gender identity is quite distinct from sexual orientation. That is, an individual's subjective perception of his/her own maleness or femaleness operates independently from the individual's sex preference.

Differential treatment towards a person on the basis of his or her transgender nature constitutes discrimination on the basis of sex under human rights law. There have been decided cases both in the provincial and federal jurisdictions holding that refusing to hire a transsexual person, or discriminating against a transsexual person in services, amounts to discrimination on the basis of sex prohibited under the law. *See* for example: *Kavanagh v. Canada (Attorney General)*[14] and *Montreuil v. National Bank of Canada.*[15]

To our knowledge there have been no reported "transgender harassment" cases as yet. However, this does not mean that incidents of harassment because of the transgender status of a person may not arise. We have no doubt that harassment towards a person because of his/her transgender status will be held to be harassment on the prohibited grounds of sex and the remedies available to the victims of sexual harassment will apply in such cases.

CHAPTER 2

EMPLOYER'S LIABILITY FOR SEXUAL HARASSMENT

Sexual harassment has both direct and indirect costs for the employer. The most obvious direct cost to an employer is losing a sexual harassment suit. The victim may be awarded general and consequential damages, back pay and legal fees (and the employer may have to pay the legal fees of the commission as well). There are also indirect costs to the employer. The existence of sexual harassment in the workplace adversely affects employee morale, reduces productivity, and increases the rate of absenteeism among affected employees. Moreover, many victims of sexual harassment often choose to quit rather than fight or endure the conditions. This results in a higher rate of employee turnover with all the associated costs in training and lost production.

Generally speaking every individual is personally responsible for his/her own actions. Similarly, employees are personally liable for the torts they commit while acting for themselves or their employer. However, common law has evolved a basis for making the employer liable for harm caused by the tortuous acts of its employees when these acts occur *in the course of employment*. Accordingly, the courts have used the principle of vicarious liability whereby an employer is liable to compensate persons for harm caused by its employees in the course of employment. Nevertheless, the employee remains personally liable for his/her actions. The courts and human rights tribunals have extended the principles of vicarious liability to discrimination cases (including sexual harassment) by holding the employer responsible for the discriminatory conduct of its employees.

The Supreme Court of Canada in the landmark decision of *Robichaud v. Canada*[16] established the principle that an employer is liable for sexual harassment by its employees. In *Robichaud*, Justice LaForest stated that the goal of human rights legislation was not to determine fault or punish those who discriminate, but to eliminate harassment and discrimination from the workplace.

Human rights legislation is concerned with the effects of discrimination and not its causes or motivations. Only employers (together with unions) can remedy undesirable effects of discrimination and only employers can provide the crucial remedies: a discrimination-free work environment, reinstatement of an employee and compensation for lost wages.

Robichaud concluded that it was unnecessary to attach any label to this liability; it was purely statutory. The legislation served the purpose of placing the responsibility for discrimination and harassment on the shoulders of those who controlled the environment and were in a position to take effective remedial action to remedy it.

In brief, the Supreme Court held that employers have a legal obligation to provide a safe and healthy work environment. Thus, sexual harassment by a supervisor would automatically be imputed to the employer when such harassment resulted in tangible job-related disadvantages to the employee. Furthermore, employers are liable for any discriminatory conduct (including sexual harassment) by their agents, supervisory personnel and by co-workers under certain circumstances.

Therefore, under *Robichaud*, an employer assumes *strict liability* for acts of sexual harassment committed by its supervisory employees, regardless of whether the employer was aware, or should have been aware of the discriminatory conduct. The mere presence of policies prohibiting the misconduct and absence of knowledge of the misconduct are not sufficient to insulate the employer from liability. Some jurisdictions have modified the strict liability standard to be knowledge based. (See for example, the *Manitoba Human Rights Code*.)

A. Liability for Sexual Harassment by Supervisors

An employee in the workplace may be harassed by a supervisor (or other senior executive), a co-worker, a client, a customer of the employer, or even by members of the general public. Harassers in the workplace can be divided into two groups: (a) employees and (b) non-employees. The employees can further be subdivided into three categories: (1) managers, (2) first-line supervisors and (3) non-supervisory employees or co-workers.

As discussed above, employers are liable for objectionable sexual behaviour by their supervisors and managers. When an employee's job, pay, promotion, demotion, layoff, discharge, or any other condition of employment depends on the employee's positive response to a supervisor's sexual advances or requests, it amounts to unlawful sex discrimination.

An employer's liability for sexual harassment by their supervisors is, indeed, substantial. Under *Robichaud*, when supervisors sexually harass employees, the employer may be held liable, even if the employer had explicitly prohibited such behaviour beforehand and even when the employer was unaware it was happening. In some jurisdictions, however, the liability of the employer may be more heavily dependent upon the actual or imputed knowledge of the employer.

B. Liability for Sexual Harassment by Co-workers

An employer is also liable for sexual harassment by co-workers, but not to the same extent as for sexual harassment by supervisory personnel. The determining factor is whether the employer was in a position to *control* the harassing employee. If so, the employer must share responsibility for the employee's conduct, when such conduct affects other employees' terms and conditions of employment. The employer is held liable for co-worker sexual harassment because an harassing employee's conduct can and does have a serious impact on a co-worker's ability to successfully perform his/her job. Thus, co-worker sexual harassment can lead to the same results as sexual harassment by a supervisor. Though co-worker harassment may not lead to *quid pro quo* or adverse job-related consequences, it nonetheless poisons the work environment. Who better than the employer is in a position to provide a healthy and safe working environment?

The Canadian Human Rights Commission's policy statement holds an employer vicariously liable even in situations where non-supervisory personnel carry out the harassment:

> An act of harassment committed by an *employee or agent* of any employer in the course of employment shall be considered to be an act committed by that employer. [Emphasis added.]

In 1991, the Saskatchewan Court of Queen's Bench in *Thessaloniki Holdings Ltd. v. Saskatchewan Human Rights Commission*[17]confirmed that employers could be held liable for work-related sexual harassment or other discrimination by their employees, including "those without supervisory powers."

The decisions of the Supreme Court of Canada in *Robichaud* and *Janzen* and the decisions of the provincial human rights tribunals and courts leave no doubt whatsoever that an employer can be liable for sexual harassment in the workplace, whether it was caused by supervisory or non-supervisory employees and regardless of whether it led to job-related reprisals.

C. Liability for Sexual Harassment by Non-Employees

An employer may also be held responsible for the acts of non-employees with respect to sexual harassment of employees in the workplace, where the employer, its agents or its supervisory employees knew or should have known of the unlawful conduct, and the employer failed to take immediate and appropriate corrective action.

An employer's potential liability for non-employee sexual harassment depends upon the extent of the employer's control over the non-employee and any other legal responsibility that the employer may have with respect to the non-employee's conduct. Consequently, the employer's liability for non-employee sexual harassment is determined on the basis of the *totality of the circumstances* in each case, including employer knowledge, corrective action, degree of control, and other legal responsibility.

Furthermore, employers have been found liable in situations where the employer could be deemed responsible for creating the situation that set in motion the sexual harassment. For example, in *EEOC v. Sage Realty Corporation,*[18] the employer forced its employees to wear sexy and revealing uniforms, which made the employees targets of lewd comments, gestures, and physical sexual harassment by customers and those passing through the lobby. The employer was held liable for the sexual harassment by the customers.

D. Individual Harassers - No Free Ride

As stated in the beginning of this chapter, every individual is personally liable for the acts he/she commits. Employees are personally liable for the acts they commit while acting for themselves or for their employer. As we also saw, employers are required to provide a harassment free work environment and when the employer failed to do so, the employer was held liable. However, this does not mean that the individual harassers are immune from liability for their sexual misconduct. The courts have normally found joint and several liability for employers and harassers.

Even though a victim may be awarded damages against an individual respondent, it is unlikely that the victim will be able to recover substantial damages from an individual. For example, in a recent case, the Canadian Human Rights Tribunal found a supervisor individually liable for sexual harassment of four female employees. The individual harasser was directed to pay over one hundred thousand dollars in damages to these four complainants.[19] The individual harasser thereafter declared bankruptcy, and the victims were left with an unrecoverable award.

Therefore, in order to actually receive some compensation, victims generally do not pursue a claim of sexual harassment against the individual harasser and rather seek redress from the employer. Nonetheless, individual harassers remain personally liable and the courts and tribunals have begun to award hefty damages against them.

E. Limit Your Liability Through Due Diligence

Employers are required to take *immediate and effective* steps to protect employees from harassment, and to exercise reasonable care to prevent and correct the situation promptly. Employers have a legal duty to prevent, reduce or limit the harassment. Once harassment has occurred, the employer's action may have the effects of eliminating the harm caused or mitigating its effects to the point where entitlement to damages is nominal at most. The adequacy of the employer's response will reduce its liability **only** if it had the practical effect of reducing the harm.[20]

An employer who responds quickly and effectively to a complaint by implementing a scheme to remedy and prevent reoccurrence will not be liable to the same extent as an employer who does little or nothing.[21]

It may be noted that the *Canadian Human Rights Act* provides for a due diligence defence in section 65(2) as follows:

> An act or omission shall not, by virtue of subsection (1), be deemed to be an act or omission committed by a person, association or organization if it is established that the person, association, or organization did not consent to the commission of the act or omission and exercised all due diligence to prevent the act or omission being committed and, subsequently, to mitigate or avoid the effect thereof.

"Due diligence" according to *Black's Law Dictionary* means:

> Such measure of prudence, activity or assiduity, as is properly to be exercised from, and ordinarily exercised by, a reasonable and prudent man (person) under the particular circumstances; not measured by any absolute standard, but depending on the relative facts of the special case.

In the landmark case, *Robichaud* v. *Canada*,[22] Justice LaForest of the Supreme Court of Canada, made the following observations:

> I should perhaps add that while the conduct of an employer is theoretically irrelevant to the imposition of liability in a case like this, it may nonetheless have important practical implications for the employer, its conduct may preclude or render redundant many of the contemplated remedies. For example, *an employer who responds quickly and effectively to a complaint by instituting a scheme to remedy and prevent recurrence will not be liable to the same extent, if at all, as an employer who fails to adopt such steps.* These matters, however, go to remedial consequences, not liability.[23] [Emphasis added.]

In *Fleet Industries*[24] the arbitrator stated that an employer would not be held liable if it could demonstrate that it had taken precautions to prevent sexist conduct and was not itself directly involved in actions over which it had little or no real control. The arbitrator pointed out that the company was not indifferent or lax in its attitude towards sexual harassment. As soon as the company became aware of a specific act of sexual harassment against a female employee, it responded immediately. Graffiti was removed on the same day it came to the attention of the company. The company also circulated a memo on the problem of "offensive graffiti in washroom walls," pursued an investigation, and encouraged the union to pursue its own investigation.[25]

The arbitrator further pointed out that an employer who had attempted to address the issues of sexual harassment and sex discrimination should not be held responsible for the secretive acts of a harasser, just as an employer who had made every reasonable effort to ensure a safe and secure workplace should not be held liable for an unpredictable workplace assault by an employee, or indeed a trespasser. Accordingly, to hold an employer liable, there must be proof that the employer was relaxed or indifferent towards providing a harassment free work environment.

The B.C. Human Rights Tribunal in *Ferguson v. Muench*[26] stated that the adequacy of an employer's response can diminish, not eliminate, its liability only if it has in fact reduced the harm. The critical factor was not so much what the employer's actions were, but whether the employer was able to redress the harm or eliminate the cause of the harm *to the best of its ability*.

In the United States, the courts have allowed an affirmative action defence where (1) the employer demonstrated that it exercised reasonable care to prevent and correct promptly any sexually harassing behaviour, and (2) the employer demonstrated that the employee unreasonably failed to take advantage of any preventive or corrective opportunities provided by the employer or to avoid harm otherwise.

Employers must demonstrate that they acted to prevent sexual harassment. In *Faragher v. City of Boca Raton*,[27] the U.S. Supreme

Court held that it was not sufficient that the employer had a sexual harassment policy because that policy was not disseminated to the plaintiff, her coworkers or her supervisors. Therefore, the Court held that the employer was precluded from using the due diligence defence and held the employer liable for the harassment.

In *Burlington Industries Inc. v. Ellerth,*[28] the court held that even if the employer had an adequate sexual harassment policy, it had to demonstrate that it acted promptly to correct any sexually harassing behaviour. Furthermore, even if the employer had a sexual harassment policy in place that was distributed to its employees, the employer was not relieved from liability if it "knew or should have known" about the harassment.

In *Fall v. University of Indiana*[29] where there was a history of inappropriate behaviour by a supervisor, the court denied an affirmative defence to the employer (though the employer had an effective sexual harassment policy in place) because the employer failed to demonstrate that it took reasonable care to prevent the harassment. The court stated that the employer had constructive knowledge of the harasser's history because his "sexual harassment of women was so pervasive and well-known" and through exercise of reasonable care the employer should have discovered it.

Canadian law requires that once an employer or its agents have been notified of ongoing sexual harassment either verbally or in writing, the employer is required to take immediate effective remedial action. The employer has a duty to respond promptly and effectively with a thorough investigation as well as with consideration and sensitivity to the needs of the victim. An employer is required to take appropriate measures to protect a victim from further harassment and discriminatory action.[30]

Remedial actions may include:
- talking to the complainant;
- arranging a private meeting to obtain details;
- speaking to the alleged harasser to obtain his/her version of the facts;
- refraining from defending or condemning the alleged harasser prior to investigating the matter fully;

▸ interviewing other employees who may know about the alleged misconduct;

▸ stating clearly to both parties that harassment will not be tolerated in the workplace;

▸ reporting back to the complainant on a regular basis to assure her/him as to the steps which have been taken;

▸ in the interim, if the complainant's job brings her/him in contact on a regular basis with the alleged harasser, separating the complainant and the alleged harasser. If the complainant is required to come into contact with the alleged harasser several times per day, it may further put the complainant in a vulnerable position.

By taking steps to rectify the situation, and by keeping the complainants and respondents informed of its actions, employers may avoid further liability.[31] On the other hand, failure to take immediate remedial steps would make an employer liable for sexual harassment to the fullest extent.[32]

F. Due Diligence Checklist

Every employer should take a proactive approach to protect its employees from harassment and to protect itself from liability. Due diligence requires preventive as well as remedial and corrective measures. Decisions of the tribunals and courts suggest that employers can limit if not eliminate their liability by exercising due diligence. The following actions may satisfy the due diligence requirement:

Due Diligence Checklist

☑ Adopt an effective written harassment policy.

☑ Promulgate the harassment policy to all employees, and post a copy on bulletin boards throughout the organization.

☑ Hold employee education sessions to inform employees about the anti-harassment program and what is sexual harassment.

☑ Encourage employees to report harassment and provide easy and confidential access for complainants that bypass the normal supervisory chain.

☑ Train managers and supervisory personnel in sexual harassment prevention. Ensure that supervisory personnel are aware of the organization's policy on consensual relationships.

☑ Take prompt and effective steps as soon as a complaint is filed or as soon as you come to know of the harassment.

☑ Design an action program for dealing with incidents of sexual harassment. This action plan should include a complaint-investigation procedure and a remedial and corrective program.

☑ Treat all complaints seriously and act promptly to investigate and resolve them.

☑ Provide reasonable assistance to the complainant.

☑ Ensure adequate resources are available to fulfill the requirements of the policy and ensure that those resources are used to respond to the complaint.

☑ Take any necessary disciplinary action against the alleged harasser.

☑ Offer counseling to victims of sexual harassment. Instruct them of their rights and what they need to do to file a complaint.

☑ Ensure individuals are protected against retaliation from supervisors or co-workers during and after the investigation process.

☑ Hold exit interviews to discover if sexual harassment played a role in the employee's decision to leave. Review decisions that promote, fire, or demote employees.

☑ Be attentive to unreported instances of sexual harassment, just as a company would be alert to theft and/or other business problems.

☑ Keep vigilant for any graffiti or objectionable material and remove it immediately.

☑ Follow-up on sudden changes in employee evaluations.

Preventive and remedial actions are two powerful weapons in the employer's arsenal. Employers should be proactive and vigilant to use both weapons effectively and appropriately. The following chapters of this book are devoted to elaboration of the preventive and remedial measures that can be followed to combat sexual harassment and to limit employers' liability.

PART II

PREVENTIVE MEASURES

PREVENTIVE MEASURES

"*Prevention is better than cure*" is an age-old saying that still holds true today. Prevention is the most effective way of handling harassment and discrimination issues. The E.E.O.C. guidelines encourage employers to take all steps necessary to prevent sexual harassment from occurring, including affirmatively discussing the subject, expressing strong disapproval, developing appropriate sanctions, informing employees of their right to (and how to) raise the issue of harassment, and developing methods to sensitize all concerned. The goal should be to *satisfy* and not to *silence* the complainant. Thus, a competent and independent person should investigate every formal complaint thoroughly and objectively following the due process of law. No complaint should be dismissed summarily.

Furthermore, employees should be encouraged to report any and all misdeeds, mistreatment, exploitation, discrimination and harassment by co-workers, supervisors and others without fear of reprisals. Assure employees that their complaints will not be thrown in the wastepaper basket; they will be acted upon.

The least expensive and the most effective way to provide a harassment free work environment is to establish a preventive program.

CHAPTER 3

An employer's first line of defense is prevention. Therefore, employers should carefully develop a preventive program even before a sexual harassment complaint is received.

1. An effective preventive program should include:
   ▸ a clear and explicit policy against sexual harassment;
   ▸ regular communication of the policy to employees; and
   ▸ effective implementation of the policy.

2. Employers should affirmatively raise the subject of sexual harassment with supervisory and non-supervisory employees:
   ▸ express strong disapproval; and
   ▸ explain the sanctions for sexual harassment.

3. The employer should have a procedure for resolving sexual harassment complaints. The procedure should:
   ▸ be designed to encourage victims of harassment to

come forward: victims should have multiple avenues of redress and should not be required to complain first to the offending supervisor/employee;

▸ ensure confidentiality as much as possible;

▸ provide effective remedies; and

▸ provide protection to victims and witnesses against reprisals.

Courts and tribunals have repeatedly suggested that employers must take strong and decisive action to avoid liability for sexual harassment.

A. Supervisor's Role in Prevention

Effective supervision in the workplace can eliminate, reduce, or at least detect sexual harassment at an early stage and thereby protect the employer from lengthy and expensive litigation, humiliation, loss of productivity and adverse publicity.

In smaller operations, owners, and in larger operations, supervisors, are key. They have a special responsibility with respect to allegations of sexual harassment. As soon as they become aware of an allegation, they should respond appropriately. Supervisors should be on the alert for off-colour remarks, jokes, inappropriate behaviour, graffiti or objectionable material. If they see or hear something that could contribute to a hostile work environment - **they must act to stop it**.

Don't wait for an employee to complain. Employees should not be required to report sexual harassment to the employer's equity advisor/harassment advisor only. Tell your supervisors, "If an employee comes to you, do not tell him/her to go to the harassment advisor - they may not." Although it is an advisable first step, employees are also not legally required to tell the harasser to stop. If the behaviour is unwelcome, it may meet the definition of harassment.

A supervisor's action (or inaction) can make the difference in the employer's liability in sexual harassment complaints. Simply having a policy that prohibits sexual harassment does not protect an employer.

B. Supervisor's Preventive Checklist

☑ Stop the sexual harassment. Handle each complaint of sexual harassment immediately and confidentially in a fair and equitable manner, erring on the side of caution.

☑ Protect the complainant from retaliation and/or further harassment from the alleged harasser or from anyone else.

☑ Where appropriate, separate the complainant from the alleged harasser, by transferring the alleged harasser. If required, put the alleged harasser or complainant on paid leave. Give the complainant the option of working from home, etc., if possible.

☑ Take necessary proactive steps to prevent further occurrences of harassing sexual behaviour in the organization by educating staff and by correcting offensive behaviour. Ensure that the harasser cannot harm anyone else.

☑ Be a role model for others. This in itself will send a clear message that inappropriate behaviour and harassment will not be tolerated. This will also give the employees someone to turn towards when harassment does occur. Supervisors themselves must have a clear understanding of what behaviour is offensive and harassing. They must show employees that they have the right to be free from harassment in the workplace.

☑ If a supervisor actually observes an incident of workplace harassment (or learns of it from other employees), the supervisor should immediately, without waiting for a complaint, take the following steps:
  • Discuss the behaviour with the alleged harasser.
  • Ask the alleged harasser to stop the behaviour.
  • If necessary, separate the harasser from the complainant to avoid a repetition. If necessary, remove

the alleged harasser by suspending him/her with pay pending an investigation.

☑ When harassment is reported to the supervisor, the supervisor should:
- Never refuse to meet and talk with the complainant.
- Listen to the complainant's story thoroughly and patiently.
- Give the complainant support but without agreeing or disagreeing with the substance of the complaint.
- Assure the complainant that the allegations will be investigated.
- Tell the complainant that retaliation is illegal and assure him/her that there will be no retaliation because of the complaint.
- Assure the complainant that confidentiality will be maintained to the maximum degree possible.
- Report the incident to his/her next in command or to the human resources department and/or a harassment coordinator/advisor (if there is one).
- Start collecting information about the allegations while the matter is fresh in people's minds. (If there is another procedure for handling investigations, then depending on the complexity of the allegations, the supervisor should not investigate the incident - only take the complaint.)
- Resolve any immediate problems.

☑ If the complaint involves graffiti or some other form of visual harassment, the supervisor should immediately attempt to locate the offending material, remove and preserve it, if possible; or, photograph and permanently cover it up if it cannot be removed.

☑ Be wary of potential conflicts of interest. In no circumstances should a supervisor investigate or handle an allegation of harassment about him/herself.

CHAPTER 4

SEXUAL HARASSMENT POLICY

Human rights statutes do not specifically require an employer to have an anti-harassment policy and/or a mechanism to resolve harassment complaints. Consequently, there is no statutory requirement for the employer to investigate and resolve an employee's complaint of sexual harassment. The *Canada Labour Code*, however, makes it mandatory for every employer in the federal jurisdiction to develop and issue a policy statement on "how it would make the working environment free from sexual harassment." The *Code* also imposes an obligation on the employer to provide an effective redress mechanism for the victims of sexual harassment.

Although human rights statues have imposed no direct obligation on the employer to resolve its employees' sexual harassment complaints and concerns, they require the employer to provide and maintain a non-discriminatory work environment, free from harassment, and they hold the employer liable for harassment of its employees during the course of their employment.

Moreover, the human rights commissions, human rights tribunals, as well as the courts, have frequently suggested that an employer should take preventative and remedial steps to combat sexual harassment by developing a clear and effective anti-harassment policy. In absence of such a policy, an assumption may be drawn that the employer lacks the commitment to provide a harassment free work environment.

A. Purpose of a Sexual Harassment Policy

The basic purpose of a sexual harassment policy is for the employer to clearly communicate its commitment to prevent harassment and to provide a harassment free work environment. The policy governs workplace behaviour and is binding on all parties. It outlines what behaviour is acceptable and what is unacceptable. The policy also provides a redress mechanism for victims and punishments for wrongdoers. It further provides the procedures for resolving complaints including the investigation process.

A statement of law in a statute does not, by itself, change public behaviour. Governments are constantly required to educate the public about the purpose and benefits of the legislation. They continue to encourage and remind the people of their responsibility, asking them to change, or modify their thinking, actions and behaviour.

Similarly, a harassment policy by itself will not guarantee a work environment free from harassment. The employer (and its supervisors and managers) must constantly bring the issue of harassment to the forefront through education and training sessions. An employer needs to discuss the policy with his/her employees explaining the purpose, contents, and what behaviour is and is not acceptable. The employer should be able to answer the following questions: What should an employee do when he/she feels that he/she is being harassed? What procedure should be followed? What action would the employer take once the objectionable behaviour has been brought to its attention? What are the consequences for an employee (or supervisor) who engages in inappropriate behaviour?

An anti-harassment policy is not merely an *ornament* to be decorated on the walls of the company president's office. Rather, the policy is a practical document. It should be seen as a serious commitment by the company to provide a harassment free work environment. The policy is a legally enforceable document that creates and establishes rights, duties, and obligations of the employees, supervisors, and management. It establishes rules of procedure to be followed and provides potential punishments.

Therefore, the policy should be drafted with great care and diligence. It creates binding rules of behaviour in the workplace. The policy becomes the law of the workplace against which the conduct of the employees would be judged, as well as the actions (or inaction) of the employer. The policy must encompass minimum norms established by law (statute and/or case law). Employers can draw a more onerous policy with a higher standard in which case the higher standard would be applied.[33]

B. What Should a Policy Contain?

The first and foremost element of a sexual harassment policy should be a commitment to maintain the work environment free from sexual harassment. The policy should send a clear and unequivocal message to all employees (from top to bottom) that sexual harassment is unacceptable as well as illegal and will not be tolerated by the company.

The sexual harassment policy should also clearly outline its strategy for prevention of harassment as well as procedures for handling sexual harassment complaints. A comprehensive sexual harassment policy should include:

> ▸ a strong statement of the employer's philosophy and com-mitment concerning sexual harassment;
> ▸ a clear and detailed definition of sexual harassment which includes examples of behaviours constituting verbal, non verbal, gestures, visual, physical and psychological sexual harassment;
> ▸ a redress mechanism, including a complaint procedure, i.e.,

guidelines for reporting incidents of sexual harassment, assurance of confidentiality, and protection from reprisals or retaliation;

▶ more than one avenue for reporting sexual harassment. Multiple routes to file a complaint that steer clear of the direct chain of command allow a victim to avoid confronting particular individuals that may have some connection to the harassment;

▶ an explanation of how the investigation process works;

▶ penalties for the harasser;

▶ remedies for the victim;

▶ a provision for appeals; and

▶ a plan for implementation and prevention that should include ongoing communication, education and training. (For sample policies see Appendix A and Appendix B.)

1. Zero Tolerance

The company's sexual harassment policy should make it known to all employees that the company has *zero tolerance* for sexual harassment. The expression "zero tolerance" in reference to a sexual harassment policy is often misunderstood. Employees, particularly alleged victims of sexual harassment, often believe that the alleged offender will be fired immediately upon their making a complaint (even without investigation). Zero tolerance does not necessarily mean immediate dismissal of the alleged offender. Zero tolerance simply means that the employer will handle every complaint seriously and take appropriate action. It will not ignore any complaints, nor allow any complaints to go un-investigated. It is well recognized that dismissal of an alleged harasser is not always the best (and most practical) response to a sexual harassment complaint.

C. What Should a Policy Not Contain?

The policy should not contain any provision or statement which the employer does not or cannot actually implement or does not have the resources to implement. For example, when a policy states that a well-trained person will conduct an investigation, the employer should ensure that the investigator is indeed a fully-qualified individual. Any discrepancy between the policy and implementation could be problematic.[34]

In *Okanagan University College and Okanagan University College Faculty Assn.*[35] it was found that the employer's action of disciplining a teacher for a consensual relationship with a student was not supported by its own sexual harassment policy. The alleged conduct did not fall within the explicit words of the College's policy: "unwanted and unwelcome conduct."

D. Relationship between Policy and Complaint Resolution

There is a very close relationship between the policy and the investigation. The policy provides the framework - substantive and procedural rules - and the investigator follows those rules for investigating a complaint.

Courts, human rights tribunals and arbitration boards have repeatedly said that sexual harassment policies are often unintentionally or carelessly confusing, unclear, biased, one-sided, prejudicial and full of deficiencies. The process and procedure provided for investigations often share those characteristics. The panel of investigators is often biased, unprepared, lacking basic legal knowledge and training, lacking understanding of harassment issues, and lacking experience in handling investigations, taking evidence, and conducting hearings.

It appears from the case law that employers have often been lax in their drafting. Effective policies must be thorough, understandable, fair and objective. **Defective policies lead to court cases**. It is often only after public media exposure that companies become willing to allocate more resources to the prevention of sexual harassment.

Every employer should have a clear, concise anti-harassment policy and all employees should be provided with a copy of the policy. Employers should make sure that they have read and understood the policy. The policy establishes a norm - a legal framework for combating harassment: it should prohibit harassment, encourage employees to complain if they feel they are harassed or if they notice that harassment is taking place, provide the procedures for investigation and prohibit retaliation against those who complain, support or provide any information regarding harassment.

The policy thus becomes a basis for the employer to take action and a guide for the investigators in investigating sexual harassment complaints. The employees, including complainants and alleged harassers, will understand why the investigation is being conducted and may not be as reluctant to participate. In fact, all concerned would be anticipating an investigation once a complaint has been filed.

Employers, knowing that sexual harassment is a very sensitive and difficult issue to discuss publicly, and that barely 5% of victims file complaints, have the responsibility to encourage employees to come forward and complain. For this purpose, employers must make their complaint procedures attractive, confidential and easily accessible. They need to develop trust, confidence and ensure objectivity, credibility and fairness in the investigation process. While the suggestion that employers should encourage employees to file complaints may seem odd from an industrial relations point of view, it is vital to making the work environment free from harassment.

In Canada, victims of harassment generally do not invoke formal complaint procedures to pursue large damage awards; rather they reluctantly complain to the human rights commission because they feel that their employer turned a deaf ear to their complaint or failed to take it seriously. Simply having an anti-harassment policy does not protect an employer. The employer must take positive steps to prevent harassment and take swift action when harassment occurs. (See Chapter 2 - Limit

Your Liability Through Due Diligence.)

If employers fail to handle sexual harassment complaints properly, they effectively force employees to complain to the human rights commission. Further, a failure to investigate and take appropriate action can lead to the conclusion that the employer either supported or condoned the behaviour.

E. Sexual Harassment by Top Management Personnel

Initial cases on sexual harassment in Canada gave the impression that the offensive behaviour of sexual harassment takes place only in small work establishments such as restaurants. Most of the victims were low paid, less educated, blue-collar workers, especially immigrant women. Most of the harassers were self-employed or lower-level management. However, allegations of sexual harassment in recent years have been lodged against CEOs of corporations, lawyers, doctors, judges, television personalities, cabinet ministers, speakers of the legislature and even head of state.[36]

Allegations of sexual harassment against the top brass of a corporation may create a dilemma for management. It also raises a number of questions including the effectiveness of *in house* mechanisms to combat sexual harassment. The company must ask itself:

- Do we have an effective policy to meet the situation when the president or a senior executive is alleged to have committed sexual harassment?
- Who would order and who would conduct an investigation?
- Would the investigation be objective and fair without fear or favour?
- Can either or both parties receive a fair hearing if the case is covered by the media? Would publicity discourage witnesses from coming forward?
- Who would implement the recommendations and who would impose sanctions?

The policy should contain special provisions and procedures, or ideally the company should have a separate policy, to deal with situations involving senior management. The policy should designate an individual outside the organization (at arms length) to receive and investigate such complaints. See Appendix B - Sample Policy Provisions for Complaints Against Senior Management.

F. Romance in the Workplace - A Dilemma for the Employer

Employees spend about half of their waking time in the workplace and therefore social relationships among employees are inevitable. Whenever men and women get together in close quarters for a length of time, some romantic relationships are bound to occur. However office romances are often short in duration and their aftermath may lead to sexual harassment complaints against the employer.

Consensual office romances can be broken down into two categories. First, relationships between co-workers - in this case, there is no power imbalance between the two employees. Second, relationships between a supervisor (manager) and a subordinate - in this case, there is clearly a power imbalance.

Office romances can become quite complex and problematic, both when the relationship is going well and when the relationship turns sour. When the relationship is flourishing, it may create a number of problems in the workplace:

> ▶ loss of productivity of the two employees involved in the relationship;
> ▶ loss of productivity by other employees in observing and gossiping about the situation;
> ▶ a tense, uncomfortable, and unwelcome sexually-charged working environment; and
> ▶ feelings of favouritism, particularly when the relationship is between a supervisor and a subordinate. For example, an employer may be charged with sex discrimination by those

employees who were passed-over for a promotion where the promotion was given to an employee because of his/her romantic involvement with a supervisor.[37]

What choices does an employer have?

Educate - Warn - Prohibit

Educate - Employers can ensure that all employees are aware of *what sexual harassment is* and *the company's policy on sexual harassment*. Employees should know that they can reject an invitation for a date or proposal from anyone - supervisor or co-worker.

Warn - Put the employees on notice. Employers can **discourage** employees from engaging in romantic office relationships. Managers should be particularly warned against engaging in romantic relationships with subordinates because such relationships are prime candidates for sexual harassment claims. Supervisors should be told that the employer may hold them in breach of trust if they engage in a romantic relationship with a subordinate. Employers could include provisions in the sexual harassment policy cautioning employees against consensual romantic relations, particularly between a supervisor and a subordinate. For example:

> Consenting romantic and sexual relationships between employees, while not expressly forbidden, are generally considered to be very unwise. The respect and trust accorded to a person by his/her subordinate, as well as the power (authority) exercised by that person in evaluating or otherwise supervising his/her subordinates, greatly diminish the subordinate's actual freedom of choice. A supervisor who enters into a sexual relationship with another employee should realize that, if a complaint of sexual harassment is subsequently made, it will be exceedingly difficult to prove immunity on the ground of mutual consent.[38]

Prohibit - Though employers can include blanket restrictions on dating in their sexual harassment policy, enforcement, may be a violation of privacy laws. (See Chapter 6 - Compliance with Privacy Laws.) However, the employer *can* prohibit romantic relationships between supervisors and subordinates. Some experts suggest **disclosure** requirements from supervisors if they are involved in a romantic relationship with a subordinate so that the employer can take measures to protect the two individuals involved, other employees around them, and the employer itself.

G. Employer's Policy Checklist

☑ Do you have a sexual harassment policy?

☑ Has the policy been updated within the last year?

☑ Has your lawyer checked that the policy complies with the current laws including the privacy laws?

☑ Has the policy been posted on the employees' information bulletin boards and internal web pages?

☑ Has the policy been distributed to all employees? New employee orientation is a good time to give new employees a copy of the policy.

☑ Has there been specific training for supervisory personnel on sexual harassment and maintaining a harassment free environment?

☑ Do your employees know how to and whom to complain to if they feel discriminated against or harassed?

☑ Do your employees understand your zero tolerance for sexual harassment? Do they appreciate that you are serious about maintaining a harassment free environment?

☑ Do your employees (especially supervisors) understand the

policy on consensual and romantic workplace relation-ships?

☑ Have you selected and trained some senior employees who are capable of conducting investigations, if and when the need arises?

☑ Have you allocated sufficient financial resources for following through with the practices and procedures outlined in your policy?

☑ Have you consulted with the Union in formulating the policy?

☑ Is the Union willing to participate in Joint Investigations?

PART III

CORRECTIVE AND REMEDIAL

ACTION

Mediation ▪ Investigation ▪ Remedies ▪ Penalties

CHAPTER 5

MEDIATION

A. What is Mediation?

Labour management and unions have used mediation for decades for resolving disputes (both rights and interest). Mediation is the process of settling disputes or differences between individuals and/or organizations with the assistance of an independent and neutral person. This process allows the parties to resolve their disputes or differences by mutual discussions and negotiations. It encourages the parties to find and agree among themselves to a mutually acceptable solution.

Mediation can avoid lengthy and costly litigation, bitterness and public humiliation by offering maximum privacy and confidentiality for the parties. No legal determination of fault or liability is made. This can be a win-win situation for both parties. However, mediation may not be suitable for all disputes, at all times, particularly disputes that are of a public rather than private nature.

In 2000, the Canadian Human Rights Review Panel recommended

mediation to settle human rights complaints. The legal profession and the Canadian Bar Association are now actively promoting mediation for resolving disputes and working to ensure that mediators are properly trained, monitored, and supervised.

As a practical matter, mediation is often a better choice for a human rights complainant. It is almost always faster, cheaper and promises less stress than adjudication for all parties. It also makes available remedies which may be extremely helpful to both sides and which would not necessarily be available through litigation. Moreover, it is easier to live with a decision you made yourself rather than a decision that is imposed on you. In mediation there is flexibility - give and take - whereas in litigation/adjudication - there is a determination of right or wrong in rigid legal terms.

Mediation must be voluntary. All parties to the dispute should consent and agree in writing to the mediation process and to the individual mediator. The parties should be informed that the mediation will be kept confidential between the parties subject to the privacy laws and any other applicable laws.

Voluntary mediation is a good option for sexual harassment disputes and should be explored as early as possible. When the parties voluntarily enter in mediation early in the dispute, with full knowledge of the advantages and disadvantages and guided by an experienced facilitator, the results can be very satisfying.

Early mediation provides an excellent opportunity to explore whether the issues between the parties can be amicably resolved before making a substantial investment of time and money. However, there are times, when early mediation is simply impractical. Sometimes the employee does not have sufficient information to proceed; sometimes the employer is not convinced of the employee's determination or the merits of the claim to believe that an investment in mediation is worthwhile.

1. Parties to the Dispute

Generally speaking, there are only two parties to any given dispute. However, in workplace harassment cases, there may be three parties →

the claimant(s) → the alleged harasser(s) → and the employer. That is, in such claims there are usually two respondents: the employer and the alleged harasser(s). Both respondents should be encouraged to agree to participate in the mediation process and reach a settlement with the claimant. Moreover, it is generally the employer alone who can ensure the implementation of any settlement arrived at through mediation.

Each of the parties may have a different goal and seek different outcomes from the mediation:

The complainant usually wants:
- the harassment (unwelcome behaviour) to stop;
- to keep his/her job;
- monetary compensation for past unfairness;
- appropriate punishment for the alleged harasser;
- apology from the alleged harasser and/or the employer; and
- to avoid any further emotional trauma that litigation might bring.

The alleged harasser usually wants:
- to protect the confidentiality of allegations;
- to prove that the allegations are false and to protect his/her reputation;
- to keep his/her job; and
- to understand what he/she might have done wrong in order to make amends for unintended harm.

The employer usually wants:
- to have the issue resolved quickly and properly;
- to maintain productivity in the workplace;
- to pay as little as possible;
- to avoid unfavourable publicity and financial liability; and
- to maintain a harassment free work environment.

B. Who Should Mediate?

Mediation only works if the parties have full faith and *confidence* in the mediator's *ability*, *objectivity* and *impartiality*. The mediator should have requisite skills, knowledge and understanding of human rights, discrimination and harassment law and the mediation process. The mediator can be internal (i.e., a senior executive) or external.

If the parties agree to an internal mediation, there will be no extra cost. However, if the mediator is external, costs will naturally be incurred. The employer should provide in its sexual harassment policy that if mediation is offered to resolve the complaint, the employer will bear the cost of the mediation, including providing employees paid time-off for the mediation process. It is understood that if mediation fails, the employer will pursue the formal investigation process to resolve the complaint.

Mediators should be provided thorough and on-going training in resolving disputes, mediation techniques and processes, as well as in the sensitivity of harassment cases. Mediators should be given particular and extensive training in mediating sexual harassment claims. Sexual harassment cases can be both delicate and volatile in nature and require sensitivity towards the issues and the parties.

C. Role of the Mediator

The basic objective of a mediator in a harassment case is to facilitate a just, fair and mutually acceptable settlement between the parties, while ensuring that the mutually agreed settlement is in conformity with the norms established by human rights laws and practices.

The mediator's role is not to arbitrate the dispute; not to find fault or assign liability; not to impose the terms of the agreement; not to force or coerce the parties to make a settlement; rather, the mediator's role is to assist the parties to *reach* a mutually acceptable settlement. A mediator may identify strengths and weaknesses in each side's point of view; and explain how a tribunal may view the facts. As well, the mediator will ensure that the parties have understood the terms of the settlement and have agreed to it of their own free will.

To be effective, the mediator needs to be aware of all the facts. The mediator must also understand the scope and limitations within which he/she has to seek a reasonable, fair and workable solution.

Mediator's Role:
- to assist the parties;
- to explain the pros and cons of adjudication (full hearing);
- to explain the merits and demerits of the mediation process;
- to explain rights and obligations of the parties and/or the law;
- to explain the remedies available;
- to facilitate dialogue between the parties;
- to make suggestions; and
- to propose alternatives.

D. Mediation Models

Every mediator uses his/her own techniques to lead the parties to reach a mutually acceptable settlement of the dispute. Mediators differ in their approach and techniques, depending on the nature and complexity of the case. Thus, it is suggested that the mediator should be given a free hand to resolve the dispute in a manner he/she feels most appropriate.

Having said so, there are some generally acceptable approaches used by the mediators in resolving discrimination and harassment cases. Any person involved in the mediation of a sexual harassment dispute must understand the dynamics of mediation as well as the motives, goals, and expectations of the parties.

Initially, the mediator may begin by conducting a session with all parties present. This joint session helps the disputants understand the process and each other's main arguments. The mediator gathers information about the dispute and the parties' positions, clarifies them and seeks to understand the interests of the parties. The mediator attempts to elicit the issues that each party needs to address. The mediator should have control of the meeting at all times. Depending on the nature and gravity of the harassment, there remains a possibility for outbursts and flare-ups from both sides. The mediator should take breaks and allow the parties to cool down.

The mediator may seek options from the parties for resolution. However, the mediator should anticipate reluctance by the parties to speak in front of each other.

No one model is suitable for all situations. In each model the mediator plays a different role with the basic goal to facilitate a mutually acceptable agreement. Mediators often play the role of a facilitator or a negotiator or some combination of the two.

1. Mediator as Facilitator

As a facilitator, the mediator's role remains limited to helping the parties keep focused on the situation and facilitating brainstorming for arriving at a final solution. This model is appropriate where the problem is reversible and works best in cases that arise from a misunderstanding or where the unwelcome behaviour results more from the habits and perceptions of the harasser rather than from selfish or malicious motives. For example, a male supervisor who constantly comments to women about their "beauty" may think his comments are complimentary. He may gladly stop if shown how demeaning his comments can be. Similarly, a manager who starts every staff meeting with a dirty joke may change the agenda if shown, through mediation, that this practice brings discomfort, and not humour, to the workplace. This approach is suitable only if rationale and civil discussions between the parties are still possible.

2. Mediator as Negotiator

The mediator can act as a negotiator between the parties. This model works even in cases of serious and malicious harassment and even when rational discussions between the parties would be difficult.

Depending upon the nature and gravity of the harassment, some mediators have found it helpful to avoid the tense setting of a general opening session with all parties, and instead meet on a one-to-one basis with each party separately, starting with the complainant. The mediator introduces him/herself, explains the role of the mediator, describes the process and ground rules and responds to questions. The mediator should then ask the claimant to tell his/her full story, listening calmly and attentively. This gives the mediator an understanding of the gravity of the harassment and its impact on the claimant as well as helps in gaining the confidence and trust of the parties. The same process is followed with each party. Thereafter the mediator may invite all parties to a joint session, or carry on shuttle-diplomacy (go back and forth between the parties) as a negotiating broker.

E. Where Mediation May Not Work

Though early intervention through mediation to resolve human rights disputes, including sexual harassment claims, should be encouraged, mediation requires bargaining over the terms of a proposed settlement. True bargaining and negotiations can take place only between equal parties; i.e., equal in terms of bargaining strength. In human rights cases, particularly in sexual harassment cases, there is usually an imbalance of power. The employer enjoys superior bargaining power over the claimant. Thus, there is always a risk in mediation that the employer may take undue advantage of its economic and bargaining power. There are a number of situations where mediation of sexual harassment claims may not be appropriate:

- when the harassing activities involve a number of victims (or where there are multiple harassers);
- when the harassment pervades the workplace;
- when a large power imbalance exists between the parties; and
- where the case may have an impact on individuals beyond the parties.

Mediation may also not be appropriate in cases of systemic discrimination, widespread harassment, or poisonous work environment. Employers should not use the mediation process merely to avoid public scrutiny or publicity of widespread discrimination and harassment.

During the mediation process, an alarm should sound with the mediator if he/she discovers:

- that the claim may be the tip of the iceberg: the symptom of a much greater problem;
- that the alleged harasser is a repeat offender;
- that there are more victims who did not come forward to complain;
- that the alleged harasser in his/her previous employment had also harassed other employees;
- that the previous employer had forced the alleged harasser to leave; or
- that there appears to be systemic discrimination in the workplace.

Thus, in such situations, mediation is **not** a viable remedial process for resolving the sexual harassment and the mediator should recommend that the employer follow the normal investigation process.

F. The Settlement

Where mediation is successful, a written agreement should be prepared. The agreement should contain the terms of the settlement and a mechanism to ensure appropriate implementation of the outcome.

All parties should sign the memorandum of agreement: the complainant, the alleged harasser, and a representative from the employer. The parties should understand and acknowledge that the agreement is binding and enforceable under law. A copy of the memorandum of agreement should be placed in the alleged harasser's personnel file, marked confidential.

1. Need For Confidentiality

It is commonly believed that a mediated settlement should be kept confidential. The mediator should not discuss or disclose any facts revealed to him/her to anyone, including management or anyone external. The contents of the discussions with the parties such as any facts, figures, circumstances, events, conduct and names of the individuals should remain confidential to the degree permitted under the privacy statutes and other laws.

The confidentiality of the settlement is a persuasive force for the parties to agree to participate in the mediation. Without a promise to keep the contents of the settlement confidential, the parties may not consent to the mediation process. There are, however, some negatives associated with keeping the settlement confidential. Other employees at the workplace are often unaware that there was a problem and harassment may still persist in the workplace. Whether confidentiality is desirable will depend on the specific factual circumstances. There may be variations in the amount of information disclosed. There may also be merit in disclosing a certain amount of information with the agreement of the parties, for example, the monetary portion may be kept confidential and the rest of the settlement made public or the parties may issue a joint, agreed-upon statement.

G. Mediation Flow-Chart

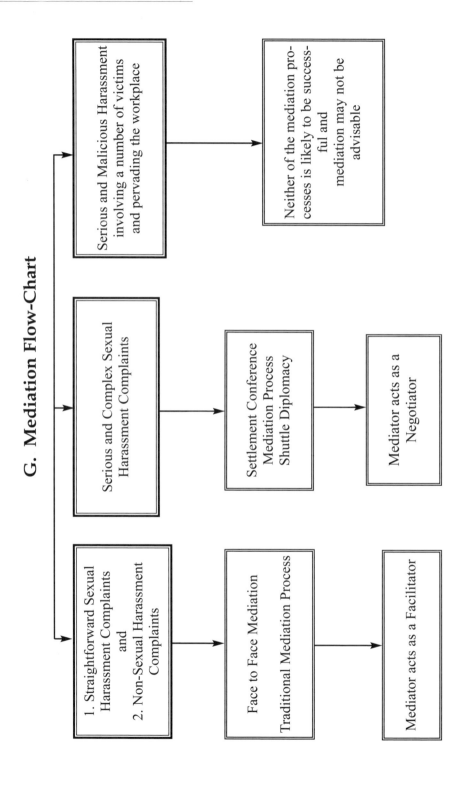

CHAPTER 6

ESSENTIALS OF A GOOD FAITH INVESTIGATION

A complaint of sexual harassment puts the employer on notice that there is a situation to be remedied in the workplace, and it places the burden on the employer to investigate the matter and to do whatever necessary to stop further harassment.

The employer's internal complaint resolution procedure can be the first line of defence for the employer. This may, however, pose some difficulties for the victim. The entire burden falls on the individual employee alone to prove the charges of sexual harassment. The victim may not have the support of the union or other outside agencies. The employer may not allow the victim to have legal or other representation, and even if it is allowed, it is doubtful if the employee would be able to afford it. Moreover, co-workers may be reluctant to testify on behalf of the victim due to fear of reprisals from supervisors.

Nevertheless, it may still be advantageous for the complainant to use the employer's internal complaint procedure if the procedure provides for an independent investigation into the charges of sexual harassment. In certain respects, the employer's internal redress mechanism is more beneficial than the other available options. It can provide maximum privacy, confidentiality and a timely resolution that victims require.

A. Investigate Allegations of Harassment

When an employer receives a complaint or otherwise learns of alleged improper sexual conduct in the workplace, it should investigate promptly and thoroughly. Generally it is suggested that an employer should investigate **all** complaints. However, it may not be practical to investigate all complaints to the same extent. Employers should be particularly careful not to ignore or take lightly any allegations of sexual misconduct. In some cases, it would suffice to provide an alternative resolution to the situation without pursuing a full-fledged investigation.

Interim Relief

Some complaints may require that the employer immediately provide appropriate corrective relief on an interim basis (prior to the conclusion of the investigation). In these cases, the employer should ask the complainant if he/she requires any type of job accommodation in the light of the alleged harassment. The employer can offer, on an interim basis, a job transfer, a leave of absence, a shift reassignment, or a change in supervision for either the complainant or the alleged harasser. Interim relief is designed to minimize the interpersonal conflicts during and after the investigation and to prevent the complainant from being further harassed. The employer must be cautious that the interim relief does not give the appearance of retaliation against the complainant or a perception that the merits of the complaint have been pre-judged.

B. Purpose of Investigation

The purpose of an investigation is simply to find answers to something that one does not know: to determine the true facts. A sexual harassment investigation is intended to determine if harassment did occur, and if so, to effectively prevent it from happening again. The investigation should answer questions such as:

- ▸ whether the complaint or rumour is well founded;
- ▸ whether the alleged harasser has committed the alleged offensive conduct;
- ▸ whether the alleged misconduct constitutes harassment;
- ▸ whether the conduct violates the employer's anti-harassment policy;
- ▸ whether the alleged misconduct, deed, or action has poisoned the work environment and how pervasive it is;
- ▸ whether the alleged harasser has previously committed such objectionable conduct or whether there were complaints filed against him/her in the past;
- ▸ whether there were other victims of harassment who did not come forward to complain. How far has the harassment been perpetuated?
- ▸ whether the objectionable conduct has been tolerated and condoned; and
- ▸ whether any employee has left employment because of the harassment.

At the same time, a harassment investigation has also some other significant goals to discharge its remedial and preventive responsibilities:

- ▸ to determine if the supervisors were aware of the policy;
- ▸ to determine if the supervision failed;
- ▸ to determine if the supervisors and managers need more training;
- ▸ to determine what needs to be done to correct the situation;
- ▸ to determine if the harassment affected other employees' morale and productivity;
- ▸ to determine whether the policy has been well distributed and properly explained to the employees;
- ▸ to determine whether the policy needs modifications; and
- ▸ to send a message to other employees, of all ranks, that the employer has zero tolerance for sexual harassment.

Remember that an internal investigation of a sexual harassment complaint by the employer is not a judicial or quasi-judicial process. It is merely an inquisitorial or fact-finding mechanism to facilitate an informed assessment for action by the employer.[39]

C. Investigation Versus Adjudication

In an adjudication, the adjudicator makes a determination on the basis of the facts presented to him/her by the parties, but does not probe for new facts or into the facts that are not put before him/her. On the other hand, in an investigation, the investigator probes all avenues and events relating to the allegations.

The investigator's function is to gather facts for determining the veracity of the complaint. He/she needs to uncover the facts and the untold story without compromising neutrality. The investigator collects information from the complainant and the respondent and then verifies those facts through interviews with other witnesses. The investigator then searches other sources of relevant corroborating evidence that might throw light on the allegations.

D. Significance of Investigation

A sexual harassment complaint is a very serious matter. Even the mere allegation of sexual harassment may irreparably damage an individual. At the same time, the well being of the complainant and the fundamental need for a harassment free workplace are also pressing concerns.[40] Investigation of a sexual harassment complaint is not a mere formality and it should not be taken lightly by anyone - the employer, the complainant or the alleged harasser. It is a legal process with potentially significant ramifications for all the parties.

The investigation should be conducted thoroughly and must meet all the legal requirements of fairness, due process and natural justice. Investigation procedures should be designed to encourage employees who witness or experience harassment to come forward and complain. To achieve this, investigations should be handled with sensitivity and confidentiality. Employees must be assured that an impartial and neutral person will investigate their complaint promptly, thoroughly and objectively.

The first step in the complaint resolution process is an internal investigation. The investigation may be subject to a review by a human rights commission or the human rights tribunal if the complainant subsequently files a complaint with the appropriate human rights commission. It may also be subject to scrutiny by the courts and/or arbitration boards, if the alleged harasser challenges the imposition of the disciplinary penalty imposed upon him.

Harassment investigations **should not** be interrogations. Investigations must be conducted in an unthreatening manner with sensitivity, objectivity and with respect for the rights of both the alleged harasser and the complainant. Only then can the investigator win the confidence of the parties in what will be a highly charged situation. To this end, and as a general matter, investigators should determine thoroughly all facts that explain what happened; ask questions in a non-judgmental manner; and never comment on the validity or merits of the complaint.

The results of the investigator's findings will take the form of a written report that draws conclusions about the complainant's allegations. Unless required by the employer's sexual harassment policy, the investigator should not recommend disciplinary action. The job of discipline should lie with the employer. (See discussion in Chapter 11 - Who Should Determine Penalty?)

The purpose of an investigation is to seek an objective and reasonable resolution to an employee's complaint of alleged sexual harassment. Therefore once an investigation is complete, an employer must take some positive action based upon the investigator's report. Remember that doing nothing is not an option and may be seen as equivalent to sanctioning harassment in the workplace.

E. Top 10 Factors for an Effective Investigation

To ensure an effective and fair investigation that meets the judicial standards as well as the needs of the parties, an investigator must maintain:

1. Speed
2. Accuracy
3. Objectivity
4. Good Faith & Fairness
5. Thoroughness
6. Sensitivity
7. Realistic & Practical Approach
8. Documentation
9. Confidentiality
10. Professionalism

F. Prompt and Effective Response

Responding quickly to a complaint may avoid a lengthy and expensive legal battle later. Harassment policies generally provide time limits for filing a complaint and for a response from the employer. The employer may consider permitting complaints outside of the time frame allowed in extenuating circumstances, such as a commission would. However substantial delays in filing a complaint may create evidentiary problems. Failure to take immediate and appropriate action may lead to the conclusion that the employer supported or condoned the alleged behaviour. The human rights commissions and the tribunals basically look for two things: "What happened" and "What did the employer do when it became aware of the situation?"

Timeliness

Human rights tribunals and courts require employers to take prompt remedial action to resolve sexual harassment complaints. It has been suggested that the investigation should begin immediately upon receiving the complaint or at least within twenty-four (24) hours. However, it may not be realistic to start an investigation so soon, particularly, in a large and multinational organization.

While it is agreed that it is paramount for the employer to investigate a complaint promptly, there is no clear definition of what constitutes "prompt action." The courts have held thirty-six (36) hours as sufficiently prompt to initiate an investigation.[41] However, waiting three (3) months before starting an investigation has been found untimely.[42] A delay of even a few days may also diminish the impact of an investigation. In another case, a court found no liability against an employer who investigated and fired the harasser within six (6) days after his behaviour was reported.[43] In yet another case, the court held that the employer responded promptly when the investigation began one day after the complaint was made and a detailed report was completed two weeks later.[44]

An investigation should also be **concluded** as soon as possible. However, the amount of time required to complete an investigation depends on various factors such as the complexity of the allegations, the number of witnesses and their availability, and the co-operation of the parties. It has been generally recommended that a sexual harassment complaint, depending on its severity and nature, should be concluded within a few days to a few weeks from the date the complaint is received. Nevertheless, as a general rule, the investigation should begin immediately and should also be concluded as soon as possible. Where the employer is well organized, the investigator is pre-assigned, necessary resources (including time) are made available to the investigator, and the investigation process and procedures are established, it should not be too difficult to conclude an investigation within a reasonable time.

G. Requirements of Procedural Fairness

84

The concept of procedural fairness, like the principles of natural justice, is enshrined in our legal system. Yet, the concept of procedural fairness is an eminently variable standard, and its contents often decided upon the specifics of each case.

The courts have held that an investigating body is under a duty to act fairly. What is "fair" depends upon the nature of the investigation and the consequences that it may have on persons affected by it. The fundamental rule is that, if a person may be subjected to pain or penalties, or be exposed to prosecution or proceedings, or deprived of remedies or redress, or in some way adversely affected by the investigation and investigation report, then he/she must be informed of the case made against him/her and be afforded a fair opportunity of answering it. That is to say that he/she must be given a fair opportunity for correcting or contradicting what was said against him/her. That said, the investigating body remains the master of its own procedure.[45]

1. Thorough & Complete

Investigators are required to conduct a thorough and complete investigation. A thorough investigation requires that it be conducted in accordance with the rules of procedural fairness, balancing the interests of the complainant and the respondent. Investigators need not interview each and every witness suggested by the parties,[46] but they should interview all those witnesses who may reasonably be expected to throw light on the merits and demerits of the complaint.

In comparison to a trial, there is a much greater margin for error in the findings of an investigation. This is particularly so where findings depend on difficult determinations of credibility, motive, and intent.[47] There are many instances where investigations have been found incomplete and unsatisfactory. For example when:

- a key witness was not interviewed. A key witness is anyone with evidence significant to the outcome[48] of the case or a

person who was vitally connected to the alleged discriminatory conduct;[49]

- relevant evidence was inaccessible to the investigator;
- the investigator explicitly disregarded certain evidence;[50] and
- the investigation was concluded without obtaining answers to the questions posed.[51]

In 2004, the Federal Court in *Ruckpaul v. Canada (Ministry of Citizenship and Immigration)*[52] strongly criticized the manner in which the Commission's investigator had conducted the investigation. The Court stated that the Commission's investigation had to be thorough and neutral to have a fair basis upon which to evaluate its sufficiency.

While ordering the Commission to reinvestigate the complaint, the Court pointed out that the investigator carried out only limited witness interviews and had prepared no analysis of the interviews. Furthermore not all of the employer's response to the investigator's report was disclosed to the complainants. The investigator also failed to include in her report positive comments made regarding the complainant's work performance. Finally, the investigator failed to address the fundamental issue, which was perceived ethnicity and fabrication of work deficiencies as a pretext.

2. Unbiased & Impartial

Procedural fairness requires that investigations should be conducted in an unbiased and impartial manner. *Bias* denotes a state of mind that is in some way predisposed to a particular result or that is closed with respect to particular issues.

The investigator should not have pre-conceived opinions about the case or about any witnesses. The investigator needs to maintain an objective and open mind. When an investigator is unable to exercise his/her functions impartially, actual bias exists. Bias also includes a reasonable apprehension of bias.

Reasonable apprehension of bias exists where a reasonable person, aware of all the relevant facts, would have a real concern about the impartiality of the process (for example, when the investigator is a friend of the complainant). Any bias, including a reasonable apprehension of bias, would undermine the validity of the investigation.

Despite of the merits of having an outside investigation, the fact remains that most sexual harassment investigations are conducted internally by the employer, usually by persons in the human resources department or by senior management. Consequently, there is a certain degree of a "reasonable apprehension of bias" built into all internal investigations. Senior management and human resources personnel are assumed to be neutral and objective, with no pre-conceived opinions and interested only in finding out the truth. However, the bottom line is that they are still on the employer's payroll.

The requirement of independence and impartiality are related. Both are components of the rule against bias, and both seek to uphold confidence in the fairness of administrative agencies and their decision-making process. However, the requirement of independence and impartiality are not identical; though there is obviously a close relationship, they are nevertheless separate and distinct values.

Impartiality refers to a *state of mind* or attitude of the investigator (or tribunal) in relation to the issues and the parties in a particular case. The word "impartial" itself connotes absence of bias, actual or perceived. The word "independent" does not refer to a state of mind or attitude in the actual exercise of the judicial or investigative function, it pertains to the existence of relationships with others. Thus, a senior manager conducting an investigation may not be completely independent, but he/she can surely be impartial.

3. Investigations by Telephone

Procedural fairness also requires, that as a general rule, investigations be conducted in person, and not by telephone. Often, convenience and economics may tempt an employer to conduct investigations by telephone; however, investigations by telephone can hardly be regarded as complete and fair.

Relying solely on telephone interviews with witnesses and

consulting documents will not be seen as a bona-fide response to a sexual harassment complaint. Telephone interviews do not provide the investigator with the opportunity to judge the credibility of the individuals and the veracity of their stories. "What was said" is important but more important is "how it was said."

During a telephone interview there is an increased possibility of misunderstanding of questions as well as responses. Additionally, it provides opportunities for an individual to make untrue and twisted statements, whereas a face-to-face encounter with eye contact provides a better opportunity to judge the credibility of the witness and the truthfulness of the statements. A face-to-face meeting generally also discourages a witness from lying or making false and exaggerated claims and sends the message that the investigation is a very serious matter.

Moreover, telephone investigation does not meet the "need to conduct an on-site investigation" requirement for sexual harassment cases. In *OPSEU v. Ministry of Attorney General,*[53] the adjudicator, while commenting on the flaws and reliability of the investigation, pointed out that "a great many of the interviews were done on the telephone." Similarly, the B.C. Supreme Court while commenting on the flaws in the sexual harassment investigation also criticized the process of "telephone interviews of important witnesses." See *McIntyre v. Rogers Cables T.V. Ltd.*[54]

Consequently, telephone interviews should be conducted only in exceptional circumstances such as when a witness' physical appearance is practically impossible or when obtaining ancillary or minor supplemental information. In such circumstances, the investigator should decide what weight, if any, should be given to such evidence. Under special circumstances, speakerphone interviews (recorded with consent for accuracy and future review) by a panel or sole investigator may be acceptable. Investigation by telephone is on very slippery grounds indeed, and drawing a conclusion on that basis alone would amount to a denial of justice.

4. Confidentiality

Confidentiality in sexual harassment investigations is vital. One of the investigator's prime duties is to maintain confidentiality. The complainant, the alleged harasser, the investigator, and only the management officials with a need to know should be privy to any information about the investigation.

It is essential that the alleged harasser be treated as innocent until proven guilty and that requires that each investigation be conducted with due care to confidentiality. **Prevent rumours from spreading**. Sexual harassment is so sensitive an area that even rumours can damage one's reputation and career. Complainants and witnesses should be cautioned against discussing their evidence with anyone - unless absolutely necessary - on a need-to-know basis. This will limit exposure to defamation claims.

5. Compliance with Privacy Laws

Under the *Freedom of Information and Protection of Privacy Act*, and under the privacy laws enacted in most provinces, employees who are party to a sexual harassment complaint can request access to information gathered during the investigation. Any party can request information such as the investigation report, investigator's notes, and witness statements. Such information can be used to argue that the investigation was not properly conducted in accordance with the employer's own guidelines.

In light of the *Freedom of Information and Protection of Privacy Act*, it is important for investigators to ensure that:

(1) the respondent is provided with a copy of the complaint;

(2) the respondent has had an opportunity to respond to the complaint;

(3) all interviews are documented;

(4) witnesses are told that all information they provide will be kept confidential (to the degree permitted by law), howev-

er, information they provide concerning another person may be given to that person; and

(5) they follow the investigation guidelines outlined in the employer's sexual harassment policy.

The federal government has also enacted the *Personal Information Protection and Electronic Documents Act (PIPED Act)*, and the provinces are expected to enact substantially similar privacy legislation. The provinces and territories are to regulate the personal information management practices of organizations operating within their borders, provided that they have in place legislation similar to the PIPED Act. If a province does not enact legislation similar to the PIPED Act, then both the provincial law and the Federal Act (PIPED Act) will operate concurrently.

In a 2002 decision, the Federal Court of Appeal[55] held that the interest of the respondent and that of the public mandated the disclosure of the names of the interviewees. The Court stated:

> The public interest in the disclosure is to ensure fairness in the conduct of administrative inquiries. Whatever the rules of procedural propriety applicable in a given case, fairness will generally require that witnesses not be given a blank cheque and that persons against whom unfavourable views are expressed be given the opportunity to be informed of such views, to challenge their accuracy and to correct them if need be.

The Court cited with approval from the Treasury Board manual on privacy and data protection:

> Except as provided in paragraphs 3(e) and (h) of the Act, the name of the source and the information or opinion about the individual cannot be exempted. Any other personal information about the source, (e.g. address, title, nationality, etc.), must be severed before the record is disclosed. The name of a source and his or her opinions may, of course, be withheld if they qualify for exemption on other grounds.

The Court further cited from the Treasury Board's Memorandum:

> [C]omplainants, respondents and other involved parties, have the right to know what was said about them and by whom.

That Memorandum added:

> All persons being interviewed during the course of a harassment investigation must be informed that information they provide concerning another may be provided to that person. Given this, it is important that absolute promises of confidentiality not be made.

There are a number of privacy statutes that may impact an organization, and employers should check with their lawyer about the specific privacy laws that apply to their organization and their implications.

CHAPTER 7

A. When, Where and Why Were Investigations Found Faulty?

A flawed investigation is not only unfair to the parties; it also undermines the credibility of the employer and the investigation process. A flawed investigation subjects the employer to potentially costly lawsuits, negative publicity, embarrassment and loss of credibility among its workforce. Employers may find themselves in hot water if a court or tribunal holds that the investigation lacked thoroughness or procedural fairness. In contrast, a properly conducted investigation can result in a healthy working environment and minimize the employer's liability.

In the absence of legislative guidance or a standard for an investigation in a discrimination or harassment complaint, the courts and adjudicators have come forward to fill that gap, case by case, pointing out what an investigator or a team of investigators should or should not have done and thereby laying down the criteria for fair, neutral, thorough and objective investigations.

Two types of cases have thrown light on what will be considered flawed and faulty investigations in harassment and discrimination complaints: (1) Employers' investigations - where the alleged harasser claims wrongful dismissal following from the employer's faulty investigation; and (2) Commissions' investigations - where the complainant challenges the commission's decision not to send the complaint to the human rights tribunal. These cases provide guidance and standards useful for an effective and objective investigation process.

B. Employers' Investigations

The development of guidelines and statutory provisions and the increase of sexual harassment complaints have made employers painfully aware of potential liability when employees are sexually harassed. That said, there is another side to the issue. Employers are being held liable for damages to the alleged harasser when the allegations of sexual harassment are found to be **false** or the employer over-reacts. Without adequate internal procedures and investigation methods, an employee who is unjustly terminated for alleged sexual harassment may have a legal cause of action against the employing corporation.

An allegation of sexual harassment is a serious matter that has the power to jeopardize the alleged harasser's professional reputation, job assignments and family relationships. An employer must consider each complaint of sexual harassment sincerely and with caution.

There has been a rise in the number of lawsuits filed by falsely accused harassers. On receipt of a sexual harassment complaint, an employer should not hastily (without making a proper investigation) fire an alleged harasser to satisfy the complainant and to avoid adverse publicity. The employer may find itself between a rock and a hard place upon the receipt of a sexual harassment complaint. If the employer is slow to take action, he/she risks a human rights complaint from the complainant for not acting; if the employer acts too hastily in punishing an alleged harasser, he/she may face a lawsuit for wrongful dismissal.

Court actions of this nature may generate awards (and costs) in the hundreds of thousands of dollars.

Experts agree that the best course of action for the employer is to have a fair, thorough, and good-faith investigation *before* any disciplinary action is taken. Of course, in the meantime, the employer must take necessary steps to prevent the complainant from suffering any further harassment.

In *School District No. 33 v. Chilliwack Teachers' Association,*[56] the arbitrator, in exonerating the grievor from the allegations of sexual harassment, stated that management had failed to properly investigate the complaint made by a student. The investigator had no training or experience in investigating, and the complainant never made a written statement or attended a meeting. Further, the grievor was given no information about the alleged incident or the complainant involved.

In *McIntyre v. Rogers Cable T.V. Ltd.,*[57] the B.C. Supreme Court found that the sexual harassment investigation was full of flaws and inadequacies. The Court noted the following shortcomings in the investigation:

> ▸ failing to separate the harassment complaint from the principal complaint;
> ▸ conducting only telephone interviews of important witnesses;
> ▸ not taking witness statements in writing, including that of the complainant and the alleged harasser;
> ▸ not conducting interviews of the prime independent witness;
> ▸ not making inquiries as to the working relationship between the complainant and the alleged harasser;
> ▸ maintaining a poor record of the investigation;
> ▸ deciding even before meeting with the alleged harasser what the discipline would be;
> ▸ not questioning the complainant's credibility at any time, despite the obvious concern that she might be making spurious allegations to further her own ambition; and

▶ failing to check whether there was a pattern of harassment that would justify the extreme discipline imposed.

In another case, *Shiels v. Saskatchewan Government Insurance*,[58] a company executive of ten years' seniority was hastily dismissed for allegedly sexually harassing a fellow female employee. The Saskatchewan Court of Queen's Bench commenting on the wrongful dismissal of the plaintiff pointed out that the plaintiff had not been given a proper opportunity to advance his side of the story before the decision to summarily dismiss him was made.

In *Hewes v. City of Etobicoke*,[59] the Ontario Court (General Division) awarded $180,000 to the alleged harasser in damages for wrongful dismissal. In this case, the employer accepted the truthfulness of the allegations of sexual harassment without a thorough and proper investigation. The Court had serious doubts as to the credibility of at least one of the complainants, who the court believed had animosity towards the alleged harasser.

In *Maclean v. Canada (Treasury Board)*,[60] the alleged harasser, was not provided with a written copy of the specific allegations made against him and was forced to obtain a copy of the allegations through the *Access to Information Act*. The adjudicator, commenting on the employer's failure to provide the grievor with a copy of the allegations, stated:

> I find it very disturbing that an employee can be charged with having committed certain offences by his employer and then he is forced to go through hoops and over hurdles to get a copy of the same. It seems to me that it is a rudimentary principle of justice that one has a right to be informed of the specific charges being made against him or her.

The same adjudicator had addressed a similar situation with the same government department in *Gravel v. Canada (Treasury Board)*[61], where he said:

> It is incredible that the grievor was not presented with a copy of the complaint. It is also ironic that the

> department terminated the grievor, in large measure,
> for violating the departmental policy while *the
> department violated the policy itself in terms of not
> affording the grievor what could be considered a very
> basic right.* [Emphasis added]

In *Gravel*, the complainant had filed a 34-page harassment complaint against the grievor. Although he was informed of the complaint, the grievor was never provided with a copy of it. In fact, his counsel was unable to get a copy and had to file a request under the *Access to Information Act*. He finally obtained a copy six months later.

In *Samra v. Treasury Board (Indian and Northern Affairs)*[62] the Public Service Staff Relations Board rejected the report of the investigating committee. It held that the investigation was flawed because certain members of the investigating committee were biased. In that case the grievor was dismissed for personally and sexually harassing a female employee. The harassment officer, who initially heard and received the complaint, subsequently chaired the investigating committee. It was the first time that she had ever chaired or even been involved in a full-scale, formal investigation. The alleged harasser was never given a copy of the complaint. Furthermore, there were some specific differences between the complainant's initial statement and the statement of allegations she signed a month later. **The evidence revealed that the subsequent statement of allegations was drafted with the assistance of the investigating committee and then signed by the complainant.**

In *Yeomans v Simon Fraser University,*[63] the head of the security department was dismissed after an internal investigation into an alleged sexual misconduct. The alleged harasser then filed a suit for wrongful dismissal. The B.C. Supreme Court found that the investigator's findings were not reliable as they were full of errors and misleading statements. Furthermore, the investigator neither followed the due process of law nor the principles of natural justice. For example:

- The complainant was not interviewed. (The investigator simply accepted the complainant's written statement as true. The court found that the complainant's statement was incorrect in several aspects.)

- The alleged harasser was not given a copy of the complaint.
- The alleged harasser was not interviewed.

Judge Williamson, while holding that the dismissal of the alleged harasser was wrongful, pointed out, at para. 39-41:

> *In the final analysis the investigation was flawed. The prime complainant was never interviewed. The statement which she provided was inaccurate.* The other most important witness, Ida Herbert, who provided a statement only on the morning Mr. Yule (investigator) wrote his letter to the president recommending dismissal, also was not interviewed.
>
> *Mr. Yeomans was given the opportunity to respond to nothing other than a "synopsis" which I have found to be inaccurate.* The information which President Stubbs based his decision upon did not have the quality of credibility which he testified he expected.
>
> *The significance of the flawed process of investigation is that Dr. Stubbs made his decision on the basis of facts that do not stand up to scrutiny.*
>
> [Emphasis added]

In another case involving Simon Fraser University ("SFU"),[64] swim coach Liam Donnelly was fired over sexual harassment charges after an internal investigation. This was a classic example of a flawed investigation that drew nationwide media attention and cost the university president his job. The investigation was found to be wholly inadequate, faulty, unfair, biased, and prejudiced against the accused. Even the appointment and selection of panel members of the Investigating Committee was found to have been biased.

Further undermining the credibility of the investigation was the fact that the complainant had gone on a four-day river-rafting holiday with the harassment coordinator and her family while the case was pending.

When the harassment coordinator was instructed to limit connections with the complainant, the complainant threatened to commit suicide if deprived of the companionship of her "best friend." Furthermore, the complainant was allowed to introduce new charges after the last investigation hearing in violation of the SFU sexual harassment policy, and the investigating Panel then relied on those new charges, even though the alleged harasser was never informed of them.

Moreover, a copy of the preliminary version of the Panel's report was given in advance to the complainant, thereby directly compromising the independence and neutrality of the investigation process. The Panel further lost its integrity by ignoring obvious facts and misjudging the credibility of the complainant.

After the story became public, the *Donnelly* case was resolved by mediation. The university admitted that Mr. Donnelly was treated unfairly by the investigation process and recognized the violation of due process and natural justice. All the charges against him were withdrawn and he was honourably reinstated, and his legal costs paid for by the university.

Whereas, the Alberta Court of Queen's Bench in *Leach v. Canadian Blood Services*,[65] expressed satisfaction with the process of investigation that was conducted into the allegations of sexual harassment. The court while upholding the dismissal of the alleged harasser observed, at para. 155:

> I was impressed by the fairness and thoroughness of the rest of the investigation. Mr. Leach was notified about the complaint; given a copy of the Harassment Policy to review; given time to ponder about his position before the next meeting; given a copy of the complaint; given the opportunity to respond to the e-mail; given an opportunity to respond to the written complaint, and he was asked, right from the beginning, whether he wanted to have his legal counsel attend the meetings. Detailed minutes of the meeting were kept.

These cases further reinforce: (1) the importance of a thorough, fair and objective investigation before disciplining the alleged harasser, (2) that the employer also has a responsibility to the alleged harasser, and (3) that a rash and emotional reaction to the allegations may lead to serious financial implications.

The investigators must be independent persons, i.e., removed from the direct control of and supervision over the complainant and the alleged harasser. They should be neutral and objective. They should be knowledgeable in the techniques of investigating as well as in the law and practice of harassment investigations.

Employers have a legal duty to prevent sexual harassment by adopting an effective anti-harassment policy and by investigating any possible instances of harassment, regardless of how the employer learned of the harassment, and even if no formal complaint has been made. The workplace sexual harassment policy should make it clear that an investigation must be conducted in an unbiased manner, as both the complainant and the alleged harasser are entitled to a fair hearing.

Although the parties to a complaint count on the investigator to get it right the employer alone is responsible for the consequences of a faulty investigation. Thus, it is important that an investigation into the allegations of sexual harassment be **objective**, **thorough** and **complete**, with due regard to the credibility of witnesses and observation of **due process**. Trained and experienced persons must conduct the investigation. The investigation committee must maintain a neutral position and guard itself against any premature decisions. Some organizations (particularly in the public sector) often contract out the investigations of sexual harassment complaints to outside agencies. Employers cannot shirk their responsibility by this process: They are ultimately accountable for the shortcomings in the investigation regardless of who may have conducted it.

Analysis

Internal investigations in particular, have come under serious criticism. The two main areas of criticism revolve around (1) not having the right person do the investigation; and (2) not following due process and procedural fairness. Some of the problems frequently cited with internal investigations are:

- ▶ internal investigators are not adequately trained;
- ▶ outside contractors hired to investigate harassment complaints are generally not perceived as independent third parties;
- ▶ failure to disclose the allegations to the alleged harasser (in the federal public service, for example, alleged harassers are continuously being made to acquire information through the *Access to Information Act* and not through the normal practice of disclosure.) See *MacLean v. Treasury Board;*[66]
- ▶ failing to investigate promptly upon learning of the harassment;
- ▶ having preconceived opinions on the validity of the complaint;
- ▶ failure to interview all relevant witnesses;
- ▶ failure to keep an accurate record of witness statements;
- ▶ failure to assess the credibility of the witnesses;
- ▶ failure to properly document the results of the investigation;
- ▶ failure to provide the parties with the opportunity and the information needed to properly defend themselves;
- ▶ failure to share progress and decisions with the parties; and
- ▶ failure to take appropriate remedial action.

C. Commissions' Investigations

The second types of cases are those, (particularly in the Federal jurisdiction) where a complainant challenges, through judicial review, the refusal of the human rights commission to refer the complaint to a tribunal for adjudication (i.e., complaint dismissed after investigation). The human rights commission, in such cases, justifies its decision on the report of the investigator. This has brought the commission's own investigative process under scrutiny by the courts.

The *Canadian Human Rights Act* requires that once a complaint is filed with the Commission, an investigator from the Commission shall investigate the complaint and submit his/her findings in a report to the Commission. On receipt of the investigator's report, if the Commission is satisfied, "having regard to all the circumstances of the complaint," that an inquiry is warranted, it may refer the complaint to the Tribunal for adjudication. On the other hand, if the Commission is satisfied that "having regard to all the circumstances of the complaint," an inquiry is not warranted, it shall dismiss the complaint.

The Commission's decision whether to refer a complaint to the Tribunal or not is based largely on the findings of the investigation contained in its investigator's report. It is evident that the Commission has no other basis to make this decision, other than on the investigator's report.

The Commission's decision not to refer a complaint to the Tribunal has been frequently challenged by complainants in the courts. The courts, in making their determination whether the Commission exercised its discretion properly have turned to the Commission's investigation report and the facts of the investigation itself. Courts in a number of cases have commented that the Commission must adhere to procedural fairness requirements and that the investigation conducted by the Commission's investigator must satisfy at least two conditions: neutrality and thoroughness.

It may be noted that the *Canadian Human Rights Act* does not provide any legislative guidance regarding the conduct of investigations. As mentioned earlier, this vacuum has been filled by the courts piece by piece, case by case, by stating what an investigator should or should not do while investigating a complaint of a human rights violation. The Commissions' investigations have come under scrutiny by the courts and have been found to be flawed in a number for cases. For example, see the following cases: *Slattery v. Canadian Human Rights Commission,*[67] *Miller v. Canada,*[68] *Charleston v. Canada,*[69] *Grover v. National Research Council,*[70] *Singh v. Canada* (Attorney General),[71] and

Ruckpaul v. Canada (Ministry of Citizenship and Immigration).[72] The standard for investigations conducted by the Canadian Human Rights Commission generally applies to all human rights commissions. That said, there is no reason why the same standard for investigations should not be applied to employers when they investigate a human rights complaint. As a matter of fact, the courts and adjudicators have endorsed that view by requiring employers to conduct thorough, neutral, fair, and timely investigations of harassment and human rights violations.

PART IV

INVESTIGATION MODELS

CHAPTER **8**

This chapter discusses the various choices that are available to employers for selecting an investigation process for harassment complaints. Depending upon the nature, size and complexity of the organization and the severity of allegations, one or more models may be suitable for a given claim.

Investigations can take different formats. They can be internal or external, formal or informal. The type of investigation is sometimes dictated by the policy and at other times dependent upon the circumstances of the case. In any event, the employer alone is responsible for having the workplace harassment complaint investigated.

Even where there is a union, the investigation is generally viewed as the employer's responsibility either because the union does not want to share responsibility or was not invited to participate in the investigation.

A. Informal Investigation Process

When an employee brings offensive conduct to the employer's attention (or the employer notices the behaviour him/herself), the employer is put on notice that a possible violation of human rights has occurred. As we discussed earlier, even though no formal written complaint is filed, the employer has an obligation to make inquiries and determine the veracity of the allegations.

The informal process generally requires interviewing the complainant, the alleged harasser, and any other relevant witnesses. Reviewing the personnel files of the parties may also be worthwhile in order to determine whether there is any evidence of prior friction between the parties.

Once it is ascertained that sexual harassment did take place, the designated officer (or supervisor) attempts to resolve the complaint through appropriate action, i.e., conciliation/mediation, to the satisfaction of the parties, particularly to the satisfaction of the complainant, and takes steps to ensure that the harassment ceases. If the matter is not resolved informally and the issue is serious, the complainant should be encouraged to file a formal complaint. Once a formal complaint is filed, a formal investigation should be launched without loss of time.

The wishes of the alleged victim of harassment should be taken into consideration in determining whether the investigation is formal or informal. It is important that the complainant feel comfortable with the process. A complainant may, for some reason, insist that the alleged harasser not be informed of the allegations and/or may not want an investigation to be made into the allegations. Although the complainant may not be seeking a remedy, the employer cannot allow harassment to continue unchecked. In fact, the employer may incur liability if it accedes to this request. Employers have an obligation to provide a work environment free of harassment and that obligation cannot be achieved by honouring the wishes of the complainant "not to make an investigation." The employer should inform the complainant that the employer has a legal obligation to maintain a harassment free work environment and that entails conducting an investigation into the allegations.

B. Formal Investigation Process

When a complaint is not satisfactorily resolved through the informal process, a formal investigation is undertaken. Of course, the formal investigation process may be pursued in the first instance as well.

A formal investigation may be conducted either by a single investigator, a team of two investigators, or by a committee of three persons. An investigator may be someone from within the organization or an outsider. As the employer is ultimately responsible for the acts of the investigator, the employer should be very careful in choosing a good one.

In a formal investigation, there is a written complaint that is **signed** by the complainant. A copy of the complaint should be provided to the alleged harasser. The alleged harasser should be given an opportunity to present his/her side of the story. In a formal investigation, legal counsel or union representation should be allowed for any of the parties who wish it. (See discussion under Chapter 9 - Request for Legal or Union Representation.)

Upon completing the investigation, the employer should communicate its findings and intended actions to the complainant and the alleged harasser. If the investigator finds that harassment occurred, the harasser will be subjected to appropriate disciplinary action and the complainant may receive appropriate remedies. If the investigation does not substantiate the complaint, it will be dismissed.

Where the employer has initiated action, whether by investigating the complaint, or by warning/counseling the harasser, it must be sure to inform the complainant of the steps being taken to deal with the complaint. Failure to inform the complainant of management's actions can result in the employer being held liable for the sexual harassment if the complainant meanwhile resigns in frustration believing that the employer is doing nothing to stop the harassment, even though the employer may have done everything possible.[73]

C. Informal Versus Formal Investigation

Generally speaking, an informal resolution of harassment complaints is preferred over the formal structured process, unless the allegations are serious or for some reason the complainant insist on the formal process.

In an informal process, the complainant and the alleged harasser may both feel more relaxed and willing to cooperate in the investigation and in finding a solution and/or a compromise to settle the matter; whereas in a formal setting, the parties may feel threatened and intimidated simply by the process itself. Moreover, the informal process being less structured is less costly.

As the purpose of an investigation of this nature is to combat harassment rather than to punish the harasser, an informal and cooperative atmosphere is more conducive and desirable. An expeditious resolution should be the prime consideration and not the observation of *legal technicalities* of the process (although, of course, this does not mean one ignores procedural fairness).

The informal process will promote understanding, better ensure confidentiality and encourage the resolution of the matter through conciliation/mediation. On the other hand, a formal process is usually structured and more legalistic. Both the complainant and the alleged harasser may feel uncomfortable proceeding without the assistance of legal counsel. This puts added stress and hardship on the complainant (and the alleged harasser) who may not have the facilities and resources for legal counsel.

However, there are a number of situations where the informal investigation process may not be appropriate, such as the following:

(1) when allegations of sexual harassment are serious and complex i.e., sexual assault, on-off consensual sexual relationship;

(2) when the harassing activities involve a number of victims;

(3) when it pervades the workplace;

(4) when a large power imbalance exists between the parties; and

(5) when the case may have an impact on individuals beyond the parties.

D. Who Should Investigate?

Investigation into a sexual harassment complaint is not purely a private matter. It has far reaching legal implications in determining the employer's liability as well as in restoring employees' confidence in the internal dispute resolution process.

Employers should take special care in determining who will conduct the investigation. Both parties generally have concerns about whose interest is at stake when the investigator is an employee of the company. The employer must balance the pros and cons of an external versus an internal investigator based on the type of organization and on the nature and severity of the allegations. The goal is to select an individual or a group of individuals that are neutral, objective, and impartial.

More than one individual can conduct an investigation into a complaint of harassment. In some situations, a male/female team of investigators may be more effective. An investigator team with a note-taker (helper) has been found beneficial. In a large unionized workplace, a tri-partite investigation committee consisting of representation from the employer, the union and a neutral chair has been found very useful.

1. External Investigator

External investigators are commonly used when the employer is not unionized and often even in cases when the employer is unionized. An external investigator, an individual drawn from outside of the organization, is normally perceived to be more objective and neutral than a person from within the organization. An external investigator diminishes the fear of bias and of influence from the employer because an external investigator is not influenced by company politics and allegiances. Therefore, complainants will have more confidence in having an outsider conduct the investigation.

The third party process is intended to guard the investigation from any perception of bias and to lend a degree of objectivity to the ultimate decision that the employer must make (as to whether discipline is warranted). Employers adopting such a process can base their decisions on the findings and/or recommendations of the investigation report. However, one difficulty found with using a third-party process is the complexity and level of skill required to effectively carry out the investigation. One would expect that the investigative procedures would be conducted in a manner that reflects the policies that they are intended to serve. Where a participant's expectations are raised to anticipate certain procedures (e.g., a fair hearing, use of an advocate, presentation of witnesses), and something else occurs, the participant is bound to be skeptical, and suspicious if not downright incensed.

Employers have a couple of choices in selecting an outside investigator. Employers generally retain either a lawyer or a human rights consultant to investigate a sexual harassment complaint. Both have their own merits and demerits.

(a) Lawyer as Investigator

Lawyers who are well versed in human rights and sexual harassment law and practices may be the most suitable candidates to conduct harassment investigations. Lawyers are usually experienced in conducting investigations of this nature and are likely to be perceived as unbiased and objective, and their presence may enhance the credibility of an investigation. When choosing a lawyer, the employer has the option of looking outside of the organization for an external lawyer or using its own in-house counsel.

External lawyers are naturally perceived to be more independent and impartial than the employer's in-house counsel. However, the downside with hiring an external lawyer is that lawyers are, of course, expensive.

Whenever using a lawyer to conduct the investigation, there is a risk that the complainant(s), the alleged harasser(s) and the witnesses may feel intimidated and less forthcoming with information. Nonetheless, investigation by a lawyer may add validity to the investigation, especially when the allegations involve a senior executive or when the alleged misconduct is of a serious nature and its ramifications extend beyond the individual complainant.

Some experts also promote using a lawyer to conduct the investigation when the employer wants to keep the findings of the investigation confidential. The employer could claim attorney-client privilege or work-product doctrine for an investigation report if the employer could show that the lawyer's advice was specifically legal and not simply "business-related."

An Alberta court recently held[74] that an investigation report would be protected by the doctrine of litigation privilege **only** when the dominant purpose for which it was prepared was litigation. If the investigation report was not "acquired and generated for the dominant purpose of litigation" but rather to ascertain what corrective action if any should be taken, it would not be protected by the litigation privilege. As harassment investigations are generally generated for the purpose of corrective action, it is unlikely that harassment investigation reports would be afforded protection under the doctrine of litigation privilege.

In Canada, privilege is not generally claimed for harassment reports because employers want the investigation to be transparent and to conform to the requirements in their harassment policies.

However, in 2001, the Manitoba Court of Appeal allowed the employer not to disclose an investigation report on the basis of legal advice privilege.[75] The employer's policy on sexual harassment required that all complaints must be investigated. The employer, instead of using an internal investigator, hired an outside lawyer to do the investigation. On the advice of that investigator/lawyer, the employer claimed a "legal advice privilege" to keep the findings of the investigation private.

There are serious ramifications to this approach from a human rights point of view. This case involved an investigation under the employer's sexual harassment policy. Generally an investigator's report gives the employer advice on what action he/she should or should not take.

111

Transparency is a basic requirement of any investigation, harassment or otherwise. If a lawyer (whether internal or external) is retained to investigate a complaint and the employer claims legal advice privilege, it defeats the purpose of a neutral and unbiased investigation.

(b) Human Rights Consultant as Investigator

The use of a human rights consultant to handle a sexual harassment investigation is usually beneficial. Human rights consultants are perceived as impartial with knowledge of human rights and sexual harassment law as well as the investigation process and techniques. However, like lawyers, they may also be expensive. Furthermore, consultants may not be conversant with the employer's organization, working culture and sexual harassment policy and would need to be educated in this regard. During the last decade there has been a mushroom growth of human rights consultants/investigators, and employers should be cautious to choose a well-qualified consultant.

2. Internal Investigator

An internal investigator is an individual from within the company who is assigned to investigate complaints. He/she may be a supervisor, senior manager, or someone from the human resources department.

Both the complainant and the alleged harasser may be somewhat threatened and intimidated by an investigation made by their immediate supervisor. They may feel uncomfortable in discussing the harassment and the circumstances surrounding the incident(s), openly and frankly with their next in command.

Employers often use individuals from their human resources department to conduct sexual harassment investigations. Employers often believe that the human resources personnel would be objective and unbiased; however, both the complainant and the alleged harasser may have some legitimate concerns about the independence of these personnel. In anticipation of a complaint, some employers keep specially trained individuals available and designate them in the harassment policy.

Internal investigators are less expensive than outsiders, and they are generally familiar with the organization, its sexual harassment policy and procedures, and may be familiar with the complainant and/or the alleged harasser.

A drawback of internal investigators is that an investigation may occupy one or more staff members for several days or weeks during the course of the investigation. Small employers may find it difficult to make their senior staff available for days and weeks at a time. Moreover, a shadow of suspicion will always remain regarding the investigator's neutrality and objectivity when an investigator is connected to any party, either personally or by way of employment. However, as a practical matter most employers still find it convenient to conduct internal investigations.

E. Who Should Not Investigate?

Clearly, a manager or supervisor accused of harassment, or someone with a personal conflict with the complainant or the alleged harasser, should not conduct the investigation. The case law suggests that an investigation by any one of the following persons may lead to an actual, or apprehension of, bias and unfairness:

- a person who intakes and receives a complaint;
- a person who is the supervisor of either the complainant or the alleged harasser;
- a person who has been accused of being a harasser; and
- a person who has been a close friend or associate of the complainant or of the alleged harasser.

F. Choosing the Right Investigator

It is in the employer's discretion to choose an investigator. Generally, the employer provides the mechanism for selection of an investigator in the harassment policy. There is no statutory provision granting a complainant the right to influence the selection of the investigator. The complainant does not have any right to insist on a particular individual or a class of individuals to conduct the investigation (unless there is a tripartite investigation committee). Contrarily, allowing the complainant to choose the race, ethnic origin, sex, or sexual orientation of the investigator would give rise to an apprehension of bias favouring the complainant, and therefore a clear violation of the procedural fairness owed to the person against whom a complaint of discrimination is made.[76]

G. Qualifications for Investigators

The individuals who are given the responsibility of handling harassment complaints must have a clear understanding and knowledge of human rights laws and the case law. They also require skills in investigative questioning of witnesses and research, and in responding to typical emotions and behaviours of those who file complaints and those who are accused.

Whether selecting an internal or external investigator, the employer must consider several important criteria in selecting the right person for the job.

Criteria for Selecting an Investigator

- ❏ Skill and experience in interviewing and conducting investigations;
- ❏ Credibility with both the complainant and the alleged harasser;

❏ Cultural diversification and sensitivity towards cultural differences;

❏ Impartial and perceived to be unbiased;

❏ Knowledge and understanding of sexual harassment law and recent cases;

❏ Knowledge and training in the investigation process; and

❏ Some knowledge of criminal law and workers health and safety laws.

H. Training for Investigators

The adjudicators have pointed out that neophyte investigators should not be sent out unsupervised to conduct an investigation. Adjudicator Kaplan once suggested that even a modest apprenticeship program would have prevented some of the investigation abuses that have occurred. "The employer had a duty to appoint a properly trained and qualified individual; quite clearly this obligation was not met in this case."[77]

It is important that individuals who are required to investigate sexual harassment complaints posses proper and adequate understanding and skills. Investigators require:

• training in human rights law, evidence and procedure;

• awareness of the implications of decided human rights cases, particularly those dealing with sexual harassment;

• training and practice in conducting interviews, including the ability to ask questions in a non-intimidating way;

• ability to use objective tests;

• training in workers' occupational health and safety law;

• some understanding of criminal law (in some cases sexual harassment may also amount to sexual assault); and

• understanding of the employer's sexual harassment policy and procedure.

A few-hours course or a weekend crash seminar is insufficient to train investigators. More extensive and continuous training or an apprenticeship program may be required. As discussed, human rights consultants and lawyers usually have the requisite background and training necessary for investigations, or alternatively the company may choose to train its own internal investigator(s).

I. Adhoc Appointment

As stated earlier, it is the employer's discretion whom to appoint as an investigator. When an employer appoints an individual or individuals to conduct a specific investigation of a complaint on a case-by-case basis (whether an insider or outsider), it is known as an adhoc appointment. Adhoc appointments are required when the employer does not have an individual assigned to investigate complaints on a regular basis.

Small employers generally use adhoc appointments for investigations based on need. The basic drawback of adhoc appointments is that unless the employer appoints the same individual(s) repeatedly, there is a high learning curve in terms of time and resources to become familiar with and to understand the employer's structure, operation, policy and procedures which are essential for an effective investigation.

J. Standing Panel of Investigators

Larger organizations may choose to name a panel of individuals (being sure to include members from both sexes) with varied cultural backgrounds in the policy itself for conducting investigations of harassment complaints. When a complaint is received, senior management will assign an individual or individuals from that panel to conduct the investigation. In this process the individual(s) named on the standing panel are responsible to become familiar with the employer's structure, operation, policies, procedures and collective agreement. They also would have undergone extensive training in sexual harassment investigations.

A standing panel of investigators is also beneficial because individuals on the panel can be assigned to investigate a particular complaint quickly, without any delay. The investigators' names have been published in advance, so that the question of their credibility and acceptability by the parties generally does not arise. As they are expected to be assigned as investigators, their normal workload is such that they can be relieved for a longer period of time to conduct the investigation. Also, as the panel members do repeated investigations, they become experienced over time and their neutrality and objectivity establishes itself in the workforce. However, individual panel members must be excused from investigating a complaint if they have a conflict of interest or a personal or professional relationship or closeness with either party.

K. Team of Investigators

It may be useful in some difficult and complex cases to appoint a team of two investigators (preferably one male and one female) instead of a single investigator, either internally or externally, adhoc or from a panel. Where the alleged harassment is severe and the complainants are multiple, or where the alleged harasser is a high profile personality or a senior executive, a team of two investigators, preferably external, may be most advantageous.

Investigation of a sexual harassment complaint is not only complex - it is also very stressful. A team of two investigators, no doubt, would be more expensive than a single investigator; however, the presence of two may enhance the quality of the process and therefore be worthwhile in the long run.

1. Investigator and a Note-taker Team

A team consisting of an investigator and a note-taker is an alternative to a team of two investigators. In this process, an investigator is allowed to have a helper who basically takes notes of the interviews. However, he/she is not simply a stenographer or typist. The note-taker should essentially possess the same qualifications as that of the investigator. This process allows the investigator to concentrate on interviewing the witnesses, watching their responses, body language, and demeanor.[78]

Having a helper to take notes during the interview relieves some stress from the investigator. It also gives the investigator an opportunity to discuss the evidence and issues with another individual. The investigator can confirm what he/she had understood of the evidence based on the notes of the helper. Consequently, it substantially enhances the quality of the investigation. However, the responsibility for the findings and the conclusion remains with the investigator, whereas in the case of a two-member team of investigators, the process, findings, and conclusion are the joint responsibility of both investigators.

L. Union-Management Joint Investigation

A Joint Sexual Harassment Investigation (JSHI) can be conducted by a committee of investigators (either on an adhoc or permanent basis) - a tripartite body, consisting of a representative of the complainant (it could be a member of the union if the complainant chooses), a representative of the alleged harasser (it could be a member of the union if the alleged harasser chooses), and a neutral person appointed by senior management or named in the policy.

Unions are beginning to include a provision in the collective agreement for joint investigations of sexual harassment complaints by a team composed of the employer and union representatives. A JSHI is a substitute for the employer's unilateral internal investigation. This process may be more acceptable and credible to both the complainant and the alleged harasser. A JSHI would reduce the reliance on the adversarial grievance arbitration process, and it is an encouraging alternative to both the commission and arbitration routes.

For example, a collective agreement between *Communication Energy and Paperworkers Union and Connaught Laboratories Limited* provided that both the employer and the union would investigate harassment complaints jointly. *The United Steelworkers of America*, also recommends for the establishment of joint sexual harassment investigation in its policy. *General Motors of Canada Limited* in its harassment policy provides that:

> The Plant chairperson and the Personnel director will then determine if the complaint requires **[a special investigative team comprised of both a Management and Union representative appointed by the company and Union respectively]** *further investigation and if so the CAW employment Equity representative and a Management representative will conduct the investigation.* In the event of a complaint involving sexual harassment the investigative team, if possible, will be comprised of at least one woman.
> [Emphasis added]

It is interesting to note that some employers have even established a permanent Joint Appeal Committee consisting of company and union representatives to hear an appeal from the findings of the JSHI. The parties are more likely to accept recommendations from a joint investigating committee. This not only minimizes the possibility of lengthy and expensive litigation but also improves the working environment.

PART V

INVESTIGATION ROADMAP

CHAPTER 9

THE INVESTIGATION PLAN

Develop an investigation plan that will act as a roadmap for the investigation. The plan should outline the questions you will ask; list the witnesses you will interview; list any experts you will need; and list any records and documents you will collect. The plan helps to strategize and control the scope of the investigation, so that you collect the essential information and eliminate what is unnecessary.

> *From time to time step back from your investigation plan and ensure that the investigation is proceeding as it should and on schedule.*

A. Pre-Investigation Preparation

Even before a complaint is assigned to an investigator, the investigators must assure themselves that they clearly understand their mission, so that they can achieve their goal with professionalism and proficiency. There may be situations when the complainant and the alleged harasser may not be fully cooperative. The investigator should prepare him/herself prior to launching the investigation to ensure that the investigation is fair, objective, thorough and in accordance with due process of law.

Prior to starting an investigation, the investigator should ensure that he/she has all the necessary information and tools:

1. Pre-Investigation Checklist

☑ Know the employer's sexual harassment policy.

☑ Be conversant with other relevant policies and procedures and be aware of the timeframe involved.

☑ Understand the relevant provisions of the collective agreement.

☑ Understand human rights laws.

☑ Know what kinds of behaviour constitute sexual harassment.

☑ Know the meaning and scope of sexual harassment as provided for in the policy.

☑ Know that your job is to find out whether there is evidence to support the allegations.

B. The Investigation

Once management has assigned an individual(s) as the investigator, the employer should inform the complainant and the alleged harasser that an investigator (provide investigator's name and contact information) has been appointed to investigate the complaint and ask them to cooperate fully with the investigator. Most employers may choose to do this verbally, however, they may want to follow up with a letter so that the parties cannot later claim that the employer did not keep them informed of its actions. Also send the parties a copy of the company's sexual harassment policy for their reference.

The following checklist may be used before the investigator begins the interviews:

1. Investigator's Pre-Interview Checklist

☑ Obtain and review the company's sexual harassment policy.

☑ Obtain a copy of the complaint and any other documents.

☑ Review the complaint carefully and break the complaint down into its essential components.

☑ Make a preliminary list of witnesses (add and revise as the investigation proceeds).

☑ Determine who will contact the people to be interviewed? Generally the investigator should make the initial contact.

☑ Determine an appropriate location for the interviews.

☑ Tour the work site, if applicable.

☑ Review personnel files and training records of the complainant and the alleged harasser.

☑ Prepare a tentative list of questions for each witness and documents you would request from them.

It might also be helpful for the investigator to prepare a pre-interview planning chart (sample provided below) before conducting interviews.

2. <u>PRE-INTERVIEW PLANNING CHART</u>

Organization Name: _____

Name of the Complainant: _____

Name of the Alleged Harasser: _____

Person to Contact:

Name: _____

Contact Phone: _____

Relationship of the Person to the Parties:

_____

_____

_____

Selected Place for Interview: _____

Date & Time of Interview: _____

Questions for this Person:

_____

_____

_____

_____

_____

_____

_____

3. Investigative Techniques

Interviewing witnesses is the most important aspect of any sexual harassment investigation. The complainant(s), the alleged harasser(s) and any other witnesses should be interviewed promptly. No witness should be overlooked or ignored, regardless of how minor a role they may have played. There also may be a need to conduct multiple interviews of the same witness to gather all the relevant facts.

Review the personnel files and work history of the complainant(s), the alleged harasser(s) and other witnesses. This information will enable you to determine whether the complainant has previously filed other complaints; whether the alleged harasser has previously been accused of similar conduct; and whether any witness would have an ulterior motive or reason to lie.

Information gathered by this process should not automatically be assumed to be true. Rather, this information should be used only to prepare adequate questions. There are always two sides to each story, and the investigator should determine which side is more likely to be true.

As part of the investigation, the investigator should talk to the reporting supervisor and review the supervisor's signed report, if any. Also, if the complaint was not reported to the supervisor (i.e., reported to another individual or designated person), the investigator should still contact the relevant supervisor to determine what that supervisor knew and why the harassment was not reported to him/her (unless, of course, the complaint was against that supervisor).

If the complaint involves graffiti, pictures, or other visual forms of harassment, the investigator should review the offending material (or the photographs taken of the offending material before it was removed). The investigator should also confirm that the offending material has been removed or permanently covered up.

4. Start Investigating

Once the pre-interview checklist and planning chart are complete, you are ready to begin the investigation. Start the investigation immediately or as soon as possible ensuring you:

▶ focus on objectivity and impartiality;

▶ give no opinion or approval;

▶ ensure confidentiality (to the degree permitted);

▶ investigate regardless of the complainant's cooperation;

▶ keep accurate records of statements made by the complainant, the alleged harasser, and other witnesses;

▶ keep a log of telephone calls made and received;

▶ keep duplicate copies of any documents and other exhibits obtained. Investigators must not only conduct fair investigations; they must conduct them carefully;

▶ listen patiently;

▶ write down everything said or done; and

▶ get witnesses' signatures on their statements;

5. Obtain Objective Evidence

The investigator should strive to gather objective evidence from the witnesses and not hearsay or gossip:

❑ The investigator should question the complainant and the alleged harasser in detail.

❑ The investigator should search thoroughly for corroborative evidence of any nature.

❑ Supervisory and managerial employees, as well as coworkers, should be asked about their knowledge of the alleged harassment.

❑ A witness' account must be sufficiently detailed and internally consistent so as to be plausible. Lack of corroborative evidence where such evidence should basically exist would undermine the witness' story. Similarly, a general denial by the alleged harasser will carry little weight when other evidence contradicts it.

❑ Testimony may be obtained from persons who observed the complainant's demeanor immediately after an alleged incident of harassment. Persons with whom the complainant discussed the incident, such as co-workers, a doctor (with consent), or a counselor (with consent), should be interviewed.

❑ Other employees should be asked if they noticed changes in the complainant's behaviour at work or in the alleged harasser's treatment of the complainant.

❑ A contemporaneous complaint by the alleged victim would be persuasive evidence - both that the conduct occurred and that it was unwelcome.

❑ Is there any evidence that the alleged harasser sexually harassed other employees?

❑ The investigator should review the personnel files of the alleged harasser and the complainant.

❑ The investigator should determine whether the employer was aware of any other instances of harassment and if so, what the response was.

C. Questions, Questions and More Questions

The investigator's ultimate goal during the interview process is to decide who is telling the truth. In order to assess the credibility of the witnesses, the investigator must embark on a questioning strategy that elicits as much information as possible. For that, each witness should be given time to think about each question before answering. Wait until the witness has finished answering the first question before posing another.

The investigator initially should ask each witness open-ended questions and then continue with questions designed to obtain further details and to determine whether the witness' recollection of events was credible and internally consistent. Before concluding the interview, give the witness an opportunity to tell you other relevant information that he/she may know but you may not have specifically asked about. The investigator might want to conclude by asking: "Is there anything else you want me to know?" or "Is there anything else we should discuss?" Avoid leading questions and ensure that you determine what the witness actually saw or heard and not what the witness overheard.

Let the witness tell his/her own story. Do not reveal any information to the witness. Do not discuss your list of witnesses or investigation plan. Do not try to counsel the witness, but do give the witness time to regain composure if needed.

D. Time and Place of Interviews

The location and timing of the interviews are very important and should be determined by the investigator. The interview should be in a comfortable surrounding where the witness feels at ease to express him/herself without intimidation or fear.

Witnesses may be apprehensive about having other employees seeing them talking to the investigator. Therefore, the place chosen for the interview should be as private as possible and out of management and public view where confidentiality can be maintained. A site outside of the company's premises is often preferred.

Confidentiality and privacy are important in conducting interviews. Distractions, whether in the plant, office or elsewhere tend to have an adverse effect on interviews. Some experts are of the view that interviews should be conducted at the workplace and during business hours as employees are paid for their interview time. Some witnesses will prefer to be interviewed after business hours and away from the workplace in order to maintain their confidentiality, and such requests should be accommodated. It is important that the witness be at ease so that he/she will be willing to disclose sensitive information.

Furthermore, remember that interviewing takes time. Thus, it is advisable to allocate more time rather than less when arranging a meeting. Some experts suggest that, on an average, at least two hours per witness should be allowed. Keep in mind that the time of the interview should be at the convenience of the witness.

E. Request for Legal or Union Representation

Some complainants and respondents may feel more comfortable if their union representative or a lawyer is present with them during the interview. Therefore, the investigator should not be surprised by a request from the complainant and/or the alleged harasser that they want a union representative or a lawyer with them at the time of the interview.

Complainants are sometimes reluctant to speak to the investigator alone. Complainants are often apprehensive about the investigator and the whole investigation process. They may want someone to be present for support and assistance, or they may want representation. If a workplace is unionized the collective agreement may provide for representation for the complainant.

> ❖ **In a union setting, allow a union representative.**
> ❖ **In a non-union setting, allow another person for moral support**

If the complainant requests that his/her lawyer be present, you should try to discourage it. Explain that the interviewing process is not meant to be an adversarial proceeding and that the goal is merely to collect all the facts. However, if the complainant insists, you should allow a lawyer to be present.

Employers have a right to speak to their employees or conduct investigations without interference from anyone. However, allegations of sexual harassment are serious, and the alleged harasser may not cooperate without having a lawyer present. Thus, it is advisable to allow legal representation for the alleged harasser as well.

Consequently, the investigator should generally allow the complainant, alleged harasser and the witnesses to bring representation with them - a relation, friend, union representative or a lawyer. That said, be cautious if a witness chooses a relative or a friend to be present during the interview - the investigator should request the relative or friend to wait outside if the investigator needs to ask delicate questions such as, "What was your personal relationship with the alleged harasser?" "Did you have a consensual romantic relationship with the alleged harasser?" The witness may not want to reveal the true answers to these types of questions in front of family members and close friends.

Nonetheless, it is the investigator who should decide the *role* that the representative plays in the interview. Generally, investigators take the position that the role of the counsel or the union representative is limited to observing and advising the witness. At the outset, inform the lawyer or the union representative that it is important to hear the witness' story, and advise the representative about his/her role in this regard.

By and large, employers and investigators prefer not to have lawyers present at the interview. However, a lawyer's presence at the interview gives credibility to the investigation and should not be opposed. An additional benefit of having a lawyer present at the interview is that it makes it difficult for the alleged harasser to later claim that the investigator coerced him/her to answer questions. **Note**: If during the investigation, the severity of the allegations rises to the degree of criminal acts, consult the employer's lawyer.

F. Note Taking

Another responsibility of the investigator is to take detailed notes during the interviews so that there is an accurate record to refer to later. The goal should be to record witness' statements verbatim. A detailed and accurate record of the investigation shows that you were complete and thorough and helps you remember what was said. It might be useful to maintain an investigation log to keep track of your activities.

> **The Key to Good Note Taking is Listening**

Make sure you understand what the witnesses are saying. Do not hesitate to ask them to repeat what they have just said. Notes should be taken carefully without stray commentary, just the facts. Be sure to include attributions so that you can remember who said what.

Some investigators find it useful to have someone else take the notes. (See discussion in Chapter 8 - Investigator and a Note-taker Team.) Investigation of a sexual harassment complaint is a very serious and stressful process. Having a designated note-taker can help. This frees up the investigator to concentrate on interviewing the witness and assessing credibility without worrying about writing everything down. If the investigator is internal to the company, have another management person present during the interviewing process to take notes.

During the interviewing stage the investigator should be cautious not to draw hasty conclusions, and not to show any personal opinions on the credibility of witnesses. Any such expression may indicate bias or lack of objectivity.

Using an electronic device (i.e., a tape recorder) to record the interview may be useful at times, but only if with the consent of the witness. However, most experts agree that recording devices should not be used because:

- it may intimidate the interviewees;
- it is laborious and time consuming to transcribe conversations; and
- the machine may fail and then the record will be lost.

The investigator should show the witness notes of his/her own interview and then ask the witness to check the notes for inaccuracies, make corrections and sign. The investigator may find it useful to have the witness review and sign the notes before leaving the interview. After interviewing all witnesses and considering all the evidence, the investigator should document his/her assessment of witnesses and testimony in the final report.

The investigator should carefully maintain his/her notes, witnesses' interview statements, emails, and all other documents gathered during the investigation process in his/her file in case of appeal or litigation. If the investigator destroys his/her notes it will give an appearance that the employer has something to hide. Therefore, even if the investigator's notes are illegible, it is better that they are kept.

1. <u>Investigator's Activity Log</u>

Organization Name: _____

Name of the Complainant: _____

Name of the Alleged Harasser: _____

<u>Date</u>	<u>Actions Taken</u>
_____	_____
_____	_____
_____	_____
_____	_____
_____	_____
_____	_____
_____	_____
_____	_____
_____	_____
_____	_____
_____	_____
_____	_____

<u>Notes</u>

_____

_____

_____

_____

CHAPTER 10

STEP - BY - STEP PROCEDURES

A. Sequence of Interviews

The two most important interviewees in a sexual harassment investigation are the complainant and the alleged harasser. Sexual harassment, as we noted, generally does not take place openly in public view - seldom are there any eyewitnesses. Consequently, the events as described by the complainant become the basis for further exploration into the allegations.

There is some disagreement among the experts on the issue of whether the alleged harasser should be interviewed immediately after interviewing the complainant or whether the investigator should wait until other reliable witnesses have confirmed the merits of the complainant's story. Generally, it is advisable to speak first with the complainant and his/her witnesses to get the complainant's story and details of the incident before confronting the alleged harasser. After interviewing the complainant, the alleged harasser and their witnesses, the investigator should seek information from other sources. Talk to the complainant, the alleged harasser and their witnesses again, if needed.

First:	**The Complainant(s) and his/her witnesses**
Second:	**The Alleged Harasser(s) and his/her witnesses**
Third:	**Other Witnesses**
Fourth:	**Re-interview witnesses as needed**

However, depending on the nature of the allegations, it may be advantageous to interview the alleged harasser immediately after interviewing the complainant. In the event that the alleged harasser admits to the allegations, there may be no need to probe further. Unintentional sexual harassment complaints based on misunderstandings can also be resolved quickly. For example, suppose the complainant alleges that her supervisor placed his arm around her shoulder. Once confronted, the supervisor may express shock to learn that the complainant had complained and says that he did indeed place his hand over her shoulder, but he was just trying to be supportive. He adds that he is surprised that his gesture offended her, and he in no way meant it to be sexual.

The drawback with immediately confronting the alleged harasser is that the investigation would fail to uncover whether there were other individuals targeted by the alleged harasser. As the employer's goal is to provide a harassment free workplace, if there is any indication that harassment is pervasive at the workplace, the employer must inquire further to ensure that other workers are not being affected. Also, if the complaint is made anonymously or by someone other than the victim or based on rumours, the investigator should first verify the allegations by interviewing other employees before talking to the alleged harasser.

B. Step One - Interviewing the Complainant

1. Difficult, Unpleasant and Embarrassing Questions

Interviewing the complainant, an alleged victim of sexual harassment, is a challenging task. Prepare yourself for some unpleasant questioning. Sexual harassment, by its nature, often involves allegations of lurid and obscene sexual conduct. Though unpleasant, these graphic details must be revealed in order to ascertain the truth. Therefore, the investigator may be faced with the difficult task of asking tough, unpleasant and even embarrassing questions in order to establish certain facts.

A sexual harassment investigation is very invasive and requires sensitivity in posing emotional and upsetting questions to the victim. A sexual harassment victim may feel uncomfortable talking to the investigator. A shy and reserved complainant may find it particularly difficult to answer sexually explicit questions. He/she may be reluctant, hesitant and shy to describe offensive and sexual details to a stranger. Therefore, before showering the complainant with questions, the investigator's first and foremost task is to put the complainant at ease and to establish a rapport with the complainant (trust and confidence in your ability and objectivity) so that he/she feels comfortable to frankly express what happened. Show sensitivity and compassion and assure the complainant of confidentiality and protection against retaliation. You need the complainant's cooperation to uncover as many details as possible.

2. Uncooperative Complainant

Sometimes the complainant him/herself may be your most difficult witness: uncooperative, withholding names and details, phrasing allegations in broad, general terms without responding to specific questions or refusing to cooperate in other ways.

In such situations, proceed nonetheless in gathering whatever information is available from other sources. It is important that you tell the complainant that the investigation will proceed and that the company will make a determination concerning the alleged sexual harassment based on other evidence, as well as any inferences drawn from the complainant's refusal to cooperate. **Remember to note the complainant's refusal to cooperate for the record.**

3. Complainant's Written Statement

It is advisable to have the complainant write or print out his/her statement. Most experts agree that a signed statement from the complainant is invaluable. It can protect the employer if later accused that the investigator ignored certain facets of the complaint. The statement should contain a detailed narration of what, when and where and a list of any supporting witnesses, including:

What happened? Describe the incident in detail.
- Was it a single incident?
- If repeated, how many times or how long has it been going on?
- Were there any witnesses? If so, who?
- Where did it happen?
- Was it: Physical _____ Verbal _____ Graffiti _____

In the case of a complaint involving physical contact:
- Who was the harasser?
  - ❏ Your supervisor
  - ❏ Senior management
  - ❏ Co-workers
  - ❏ Other
- Where did the incident take place?
- When did the incident take place?
- Describe the nature of the incident.
- What was your reaction?
- Did you complain to anyone? To whom?
- Did you discuss it with anyone? With whom?

- Did you report the incident to your supervisor or senior management? If so, to whom? If not, why not?
- Describe any harm you suffered?

The complainant's written statement also helps the investigator in understanding the complainant's story and raising specific issues with the alleged harasser.

Remember

❖ **Do not debate the merits of the complainant's story with the complainant. Your job is to get the facts only.**

❖ **Do not judge the validity of the complaint until the investigation is complete.**

---

4. What to Tell the Complainant?

The investigator should inform the complainant that:

▶ She/he has a right to be free from harassment.

▶ Sexual harassment allegations are serious.

▶ The law requires the employer to investigate the complaint.

▶ The employer will ensure confidentiality as much as possible, but there are exceptions.

▶ The employer will conduct an appropriate investigation.

▶ The employer will afford the alleged harasser an opportunity to respond to the allegations.

▶ If the alleged harasser is found to have committed objectionable conduct amounting to harassment, appropriate and effective action will be taken against the alleged harasser, including appropriate discipline.

▶ Explain to the complainant what behaviour constitutes retaliation, and that the complainant should not suffer retaliation of any kind.

▶ Tell the complainant to report any retaliatory behaviour

he/she encounters directly to the investigator. (See Appendix A - Retaliation Prohibited for examples of retaliation.)

5. Questioning the Complainant

Every investigator has his/her own techniques and style of interviewing. The investigator should be given the flexibility to interview the complainant, the alleged harasser and other persons as he/she thinks appropriate in a given situation. However, it is important to note that some general parameters for questioning in sexual harassment investigations have emerged.

Generally, the investigator asks a witness open-ended questions and then moves on to specific questions designed to obtain details and determine whether the witness' recollection was credible and internally consistent.

The investigator should first ask the complainant to tell his/her story in his/her own words. "Tell me everything that happened that morning from the time you first came to work." The investigator should listen patiently and take notes. Do not rush. Do not lead. Let the complainant take his/her own time and pace. After the witness has described the whole incident, the investigator should then go back and elicit details on each aspect of the initial statement.

Use open ended and specific questions designed to draw out more than a simple "yes" or "no" response. If the complainant becomes emotional while telling the story, be sensitive and patient - give him/her a chance to regain composure. You should encourage the complainant to tell his/her story without compromising your impartiality and objectivity.

For allegations involving derogatory and vulgar comments and expressions, the investigator should encourage the complainant to repeat the exact words used. If the allegation involves physical sexual contact, the investigator should ask the complainant to describe the events as explicitly as possible.

In sexual harassment cases, complainants are often shy and embarrassed to express or describe graphic sexual details, particularly, if the investigator is male and the complainant is female. The investigator should explain to the complainant that it is important for the investigation, that the allegations be described explicitly. Often, the more detailed a complaint, the more credible it is. Let the complainant take his/her time to describe the conduct and provide specifics. If the complainant is reluctant to say the exact words - body parts and sexual activities - ask him/her to write it down. Some victims may find it very difficult to verbally express events of this nature. The complainant's cultural background may play a role in his/her comfort level in describing the events to the investigator. Seek the help of a translator if required.

The investigator should explore further by asking specific questions regarding, dates, times, places, and locations. For example:

- ▸ What happened before and after the incident?
- ▸ What did he say?
- ▸ Where did he touch you?
- ▸ What did you say?
- ▸ What were you wearing?
- ▸ What was his reaction immediately after the incident?
- ▸ Did anyone overhear?
- ▸ Did you talk to anyone after the incident?
- ▸ What did you do after that?
- ▸ How did you feel?
- ▸ Were you angry?
- ▸ Did you report this to your supervisor or anyone else?
- ▸ Did you talk to the Union?
- ▸ When did you report this to the employer?
- ▸ Why did you take so long to report it?

The investigator should explore whether the conduct in question was unwelcome. "Have you ever told him 'NO'?" Had a similar thing happened before - if so, how did the complainant react? Complainants generally just say that they were "harassed." Do not accept that kind of answer - explore it further. Ask the complainant, "How do you know it was harassment?" "What really happened, what was said or done?" "Have you ever been harassed before and by whom?" "Did you report the incident to the employer at that time?" "What happened?" Before concluding the investigation the investigator should ask, "Is there anything else you would like to tell me?" or "Is there anything else I should know?"

Finally, the investigator should ask the complainant to review the statement, make any corrections or changes and sign the statement. If the complainant refuses to sign, do not insist, but make a note that the complainant's signature was requested and refused.

(a) Explore the Working Relationship

To grasp the situation clearly, the investigator should discover what kind of *working* and *personal* relationship the complainant and the alleged harasser had. The investigator should ask the complainant about his/her working relationship with the alleged harasser (supervisor, co-worker or outsider). What was the alleged harasser's job, nature of work, location of work, age, manners and habits? What was the complainant's job, nature of work, and location of work? What was the physical proximity of their workplaces from each other? How often did the complainant come into contact with the alleged harasser? Ask the complainant to describe a typical working day. Does the complainant report to the alleged harasser? Does the complainant have to deal with the alleged harasser on a daily basis?

(b) Explore the Consensual Relationship

Ask the complainant about what kind of personal or romantic relationship he/she had with the alleged harasser. For example, ask:

▸ Would you consider your relationship with the alleged harasser a friendship?

▸ Did you ever have a romantic relationship with the alleged harasser? If so, how and when did it end?

▸ Have you ever dated him?

▸ Have you ever gone to lunch with him?

▸ Did you ever socialize with him outside of the office?

▶ Have you ever invited him to your house or elsewhere?
▶ Has he ever invited you?
▶ Have you visited him at his house? How frequently?
▶ Have you visited his relatives?
▶ Has he ever given you a gift?
▶ Have you ever given him a gift?
▶ Have you visited him since the incident?

6. Negative Consequences Suffered

Inquire what negative consequences the complainant has suffered and how they were related to the harassment. The investigator should discover the grounds for the complainant's discipline or discharge, if any. Ask the complainant: "Why do you think that the alleged grounds of discipline/discharge are not valid?" Try to establish if there was any connection between the employer's action and the harassment. "Why do you think that you were disciplined, discharged, disadvantaged or mistreated because you rejected the alleged harasser's sexual advances?"

Sometimes negative consequences and harassment are not connected. It is possible that the complainant may be disciplined or discharged for a good or sufficient reason, and at the same time he/she may also be a victim of harassment by the alleged harasser.

7. Awareness of Policy and Procedures

The investigator should also explore the complainant's knowledge about the employer's policy and procedures:

▶ Were you aware of the employer's sexual harassment policy and other related policies and procedures?
▶ Did you attend the seminar on sexual harassment provided by the employer?
▶ Did you know how and whom to report the incident of harassment to?
▶ Was the employer aware that you were being harassed?

▶ How do you know that the employer knew or ought to have known that harassment was going on?

▶ Do you know of any other employee who has been harassed by the same person?"

> **The investigator should listen to the complainant's story with an open mind and prepare a written account of the complainant's statement.**

C. Step Two - Interviewing the Alleged Harasser

Once armed with the complainant's information, review the alleged harasser's personnel file to determine whether any similar accusations have been made in the past. Then speak to the alleged harasser. Take his/her detailed statement. Be certain to address each contention made by the complainant. Give the alleged harasser every opportunity to explain his/her version of the events. If there is more than one alleged harasser, interview them separately.

Interviewing the alleged harasser is also not an easy task. The alleged harasser is generally angry, frustrated, and resents the allegations of sexual harassment. He/she may be reluctant to talk, defensive and uncooperative. Thus, it is important that the investigator maintain his/her composure and is careful not to say or use body language that may suggest any bias.

The investigator should start by describing the purpose of the investigation and the manner in which the investigation will be conducted. Explain that the interview will not be confrontational or adversarial - the investigator is not making a judgment. The investigator's job is simply fact-finding. The investigator should also stress the employer's zero tolerance policy. (See discussion in Chapter 4 - Zero Tolerance.) The alleged harasser should realize that the employer takes the allegations of sexual harassment very seriously, even if they ultimately prove to be false.

Do not give away the specific details of the allegations to the alleged harasser right away. Let the alleged harasser relate his/her version of the events before he/she is influenced by the complainant's version. Allow the alleged harasser to tell what happened from his/her point of view. If the investigation was informal, it would suffice to begin by saying that, "Someone has complained about your behaviour and the company is gathering information." Tell the alleged harasser that he/she has an obligation to cooperate with the inquiry.

Only after the alleged harasser has given his/her version of the events, should the investigator discuss the specifics of the complainant's story. Take the alleged harasser chronologically through the complainant's story and ask him/her about each allegation and every detail. You may get two completely different stories. Identify the areas in which the two parties disagree.

When interviewing the alleged harasser, the investigator should:

▶ Explain the allegations made by the complainant.

▶ Provide the alleged harasser with all details regardless of how sexually graphic or embarrassing they maybe. (See discussion under Step One - Interviewing the Complainant.)

▶ Give the alleged harasser a copy of the written complaint. (See discussion under Step Two - Providing a Copy of the Complaint.)

▶ Give the alleged harasser full opportunity to respond to each and every allegation.

▶ If the alleged harasser requests union representation or a lawyer, the investigator should suspend the interview for a reasonable time to allow him/her to obtain such representation. (For further discussion, see Chapter 9 Request for Legal or Union Representation.)

▶ Prepare a written account of the alleged harasser's statement and have him/her review, modify and sign it.

▶ Explain to the alleged harasser the organization's policy against harassment.

▶ Tell the alleged harasser not to discuss the complaint or

investigation with any other employee (except the union representative).

▸ Inform the alleged harasser that the law prohibits retaliation in any manner against the complainant, witnesses or other persons involved in the investigation. Ensure that the alleged harasser understands that retaliation is a separate offence under law and calls for a serious disciplinary response.

1. Providing a Copy of the Complaint

There is some disagreement among the experts over the issue of whether or not the alleged harasser should be given a copy of the complaint. If the investigation is formal, there is really no question; the employer must give the alleged harasser a copy of the complaint. The adjudicative bodies take a dim view if the employer fails (or refuses) to provide the alleged harasser with a copy of the complaint.[79] Moreover, in some jurisdictions the alleged harasser is entitled to receive a copy of the complaint against him/her under the *Access of Information Act* and under the *Privacy Act.*[80]

If the alleged harasser is not given a copy of the complaint, the investigator should, at least, provide the substance of the allegations against him/her. The alleged harasser should have all the information and opportunity with which to defend him/herself. Not only must the alleged harasser be given a fair hearing, he/she should perceive that he/she is being treated fairly.

2. Consensual Relationship?

If the alleged harasser flatly denies the allegations, or if the alleged harasser claims that the complainant welcomed or invited the conduct, or that the conduct was consensual, ask probing questions regarding every detail provided by the complainant.

The investigator should ask the alleged harasser whether he/she had a romantic relationship with the complainant. (See Step One - Explore the Consensual Relationship.) The relationship's past or present could be very problematic and should be explored thoroughly. Sometimes anger or frustration caused by a breakdown in the romantic relationship may be the real motive behind the complaint. If the two parties disagree on whether or not a romantic relationship ever existed between them, probe further so that you can make that determination. When did it start? How did it start? How long did it last? How did it end? Did anyone know about it? Were any cards, gifts or e-mail messages exchanged? Did the complainant ever say or indicate that the conduct was unwelcome?

3. Ulterior Motive?

If the alleged harasser provides a defence that the complainant had ulterior motives for filing the complaint, the investigator should not lightly reject those contentions. Sometimes poor job performance, failure to get a promotion or wage increase, a transfer or demotion, rejection of a romantic proposal, or a breakdown in the romance or affair can be the real driving force behind a sexual harassment complaint.

There have been a number of cases where it has been found that the complainants indeed had ulterior motives. For example in *McIntyre v. Rogers Cable T.V. Ltd.*[81] the B.C. Supreme Court found that the complainant had an ulterior motive in filing a complaint of sexual harassment. Justice Low stated:

> Having heard Ms. Chang's (the complainant's) evidence, I have no hesitation in concluding that *her complaint letter stems entirely from her removal as a host of the March Show. ...From the beginning, she was motivated by a selfish ambition to be reinstated as host of the show and, failing that, a vengeful desire to cause Mr. McIntyre (the alleged harasser) harm.*

The Court concluded:

> However, the defendant (the employer) made no attempt to assess the truth of those assertions or to

consider them when assessing the genuineness of, or motivation for the harassment complaints. The defendant's investigation was seriously flawed in this respect.

The investigator should interview other persons who can throw further light on the possibility of an ulterior motive. The alleged harasser often names character witnesses in his/her defence. The value of the evidence of those witnesses is very limited unless they had some direct knowledge or an opportunity to observe the parties. Nevertheless, the investigator should interview some, if not all, of the character witnesses suggested by the alleged harasser. They may provide a different perspective on the situation, and would protect the investigator from the accusation that he/she ignored the alleged harasser's evidence. Secure all the information about the witnesses suggested by the alleged harasser, i.e., their names, addresses, telephone numbers, relationship with the alleged harasser, and the documents or information they would likely provide.

Be aware that even if the complainant has some *grudge* or some reason to dislike the alleged harasser that does not necessarily mean that the complainant was not harassed. Often there may be a combination of events and emotions that have led to the complaint.

4. Respect the Alleged Harasser's Rights

Never discipline, discharge, or hastily punish an alleged harasser to avoid legal action or adverse publicity. Employers are often caught between (1) the prospect of a complaint to the human rights commission or a lawsuit from the victim of harassment and (2) an equally frightening prospect of a lawsuit from the alleged harasser.

The alleged harasser should be given every opportunity to offer a response and rebuttal to every allegation, and should not be rushed to complete his/her responses. The investigator should be on guard against a charge of unfairness, incompleteness and bias. The best approach that an employer can take is to determine the validity of a complaint and take disciplinary action - *only after a good faith investigation* - that is fair, thorough and objective.

The investigator should talk with the alleged harasser as many times as necessary during the process of investigation, particularly if any new evidence emerges. At the conclusion of the investigation, ask the alleged harasser one more time if he/she has other information to provide. Tell the alleged harasser to contact you if he/she thinks of something that he/she wants to add after the interview. Finally ask if there is any other person the investigator should perhaps talk to.

The investigator will prepare a written account of the alleged harasser's statement, and ask him/her to review for accuracy, to make any needed corrections, and to sign the statement. If the alleged harasser refuses to sign, the investigator will note that signature was requested and refused.

D. Step Three - Interviewing Other Witnesses

Interview other individuals who may have some knowledge about the alleged incident or who can provide some relevant background information, such as the working relationship between the parties; previous investigations, if any; and incidents of possible harassment of other persons.

1. Whom Should You Interview?

The investigator should speak to anyone who might support the complainant's or the alleged harasser's account of events. Although, the investigator is not obliged to interview every individual suggested by the parties, the investigator should not overlook any witness who could throw light on the events. The investigator should speak to every relevant witness. For example, the B.C. Supreme Court in *McIntyre v. Rogers Cable T.V. Ltd.*,[82] found that failure to interview a prime independent witness was one of the serious flaws in the investigation.

In addition to interviewing the witnesses identified by the

complainant and the alleged harasser, supervisory and managerial employees, as well as co-workers, should be asked about their knowledge of the alleged harassment. Further, testimony may be obtained from persons who observed the complainant's demeanour immediately after an alleged incident of harassment. Persons with whom the complainant discussed the incident - such as co-workers, a doctor (with consent), or a counselor (with consent) - should also be interviewed. Other employees should be asked if they noticed changes in the complainant's behaviour at work or in the alleged harasser's treatment of the complainant.

2. What to Tell Witnesses?

At the outset of each of the in-person interviews, the investigator should explain to the interviewees:

- the purpose and process of the interview about to take place;
- that they are looking into allegations of inappropriate behaviour on the part of "Mr. X" (the alleged harasser) and gathering information which will be presented to him for his responses. Some experts feel that the investigator should not disclose the identity of the complainant and the alleged harasser unless absolutely necessary;
- that they are under no obligation to speak to the investigator;
- that they are entitled to have someone else present during the interview;
- that notes will be taken during the interview which they will be asked to review, make any revisions and sign;
- that the company will ensure confidentiality, to the maximum degree possible, however, information they provide concerning another person may be given to that person; and
- that the investigator will conduct an appropriate investigation;
- that the investigator will afford full opportunity to the

alleged harasser to respond to the allegations;

- that the organization prohibits any form of retaliation as a result of their participation in the investigation;
- to report any retaliation they experience directly to the investigator; and
- to avoid discussing the incident or investigation with any-one.

3. What to Ask Witnesses?

As with all witnesses, the investigator should begin with open-ended questions and then follow-up with more specific questions to elicit further details and determine whether the witnesses' recollections of events were credible and internally consistent.

- Ask what the witness knows about the situation.
- Ask about the complainant's demeanour and behaviour during and after the incident as well as that of the alleged harasser.
- Ask for the names of other potential witnesses.
- Ask if he/she would like to add anything further or any other relevant information.

Ensure that the witnesses had first-hand knowledge of the events and that they are not simply relaying office gossip. It is important that the witnesses provide information only about what they actually saw or heard. Ask them questions such as:

- ▸ Who initiated the alleged conduct?
- ▸ Did you actually see it?
- ▸ What was known about the relationship between the complainant and the alleged harasser?
- ▸ Have you observed anything since the incident occurred?

4. Determine Objectivity of Third Party Witnesses

The investigator should be careful of polarization. In some high profile or volatile sexual harassment cases, the workplace divides into two camps - one supporting the complainant and the other supporting the alleged harasser. In such a charged environment it becomes difficult to determine who is and who is not telling the truth. It is not that witnesses are deliberately lying, but their emotions sometimes become so entangled with facts that they themselves find it difficult to separate fact from fiction.

Thus, the investigator should try to determine if the witness has any ulterior motive or favouritism. For this purpose, the investigator may ask the witness directly if he/she has any personal, family or other relationship either with the complainant or the accused. Determine how the witness fits into the picture. The investigator, depending upon the witness' story, should ask questions such as the following:

- ▶ Are you a friend of the complainant?
- ▶ Are you a friend of the alleged harasser?
- ▶ Have you ever socialized with either the complainant or the alleged harasser?
- ▶ Have you ever worked under the alleged harasser?
- ▶ How was your working relationship with the alleged harasser when he/she was your boss?
- ▶ Did you get along well with him?
- ▶ Do you have any reason to dislike the alleged harasser?
- ▶ Have you ever filed a grievance or a complaint against the alleged harasser?
- ▶ Was the complainant promoted over you?
- ▶ How long have you been working here?

Answers to these kinds of questions will help the investigator sort out biases and determine if the witness is telling the truth.

In order to maintain and protect confidentiality, third party witnesses should only be told about the sexual harassment complaint to the degree that is necessary to elicit those facts that pertain to the witness. Do not tell a witness what the complainant said happened, because that could influence the witness and change the way he/she answers questions.

At the conclusion of the interview, the witness should be reminded not to discus anything about the interview with anyone. Remind him/her that sexual harassment is a serious and sensitive matter, and breach of confidentiality will not be tolerated.

E. Step Four - Re-interview as Needed

Once the investigator has interviewed the alleged harasser and other witnesses, examined the pertinent documents and records, visited the location and sites, he/she may require verification, confirmation or reaction from the complainant. Similarly, the investigator may need to talk to the alleged harasser again if new facts or issues surface. It is generally suggested that the investigator should feel free to talk to the parties as many times as necessary to reach to the depth and truth of the story. However, in the situation where the alleged harasser has admitted the wrongdoing as alleged, there is no need to interview the complainant again.

There is nothing wrong in re-interviewing the complainant, the alleged harasser and even key witnesses, if required. Sometimes you may need to re-interview individuals more than once. In practice the road map of any case is not straightforward - the story unfolds in bits and pieces. New issues, facts and new dimensions are raised that must be confirmed, explained and corroborated. The basic purpose of re-interviewing is to:

- tie up loose ends,
- complete the story,
- get clarification and/or explanation on the new points or information that has emerged, and
- get the complainant's reaction to the alleged harasser's story.

F. Step Five - Visit the Site and Examine Relevant Documents

The investigator should not confine his/her investigation only to interviewing the parties and their witnesses; rather he/she should try to uncover other relevant information that could throw light on the alleged conduct from whatever sources are available. Consider all possible relevant evidence in an effort to corroborate the facts reported by the interviewees. For example, examine any documentation referred to or given by a witness during his/her interview, and review relevant electronic media including websites, internet history records, emails, computer files, appointment calendars and photographs.

The investigator should collect and examine relevant background information, including the personnel files of the complainant and the alleged harasser. Review payroll records for sick days, vacation days and holidays corresponding to the times of the incident(s); review expense reports for hotels, restaurants, and other credit card receipts; review telephone, cell phone and voice-mail records; and also review any relevant medical or counseling records with the consent of the individual.

A *visit to the workplace* and viewing the site of the alleged incident can also prove beneficial. Sometimes, depending on the circumstances, it is necessary to look at the physical setting to see whether it supports or undermines the assertions of either side. For example, suppose the complainant claims that the alleged harasser brushed up against her buttocks in the hallway when she was coming from the photocopier. After viewing the location, the investigator may find that the hallway was so narrow, that two people could not possibly pass through it at the same time without touching each other. This gives the investigator some context to ask further questions to determine if the contact was intentional. Viewing the site may also show the investigator who was in a position to observe the alleged incident and if anything might have blocked his/her view.

It is important to explore all avenues for obtaining corroborative evidence because tribunals and courts may reject harassment claims due to lack of corroborative evidence.

G. Step Six - Making the Determination

The basic purpose of an investigation is to find out whether there is sufficient evidence to support the allegations in light of the organization's policy and the law. This involves an assessment of the evidence (oral and documentary) and a determination of the credibility of the witnesses.

1. Evaluating the Evidence

The investigator now proceeds to review the witnesses' statements and any other material that may assist in evaluation of the evidence. Investigators should rely on objective evidence rather than subjective, un-communicated findings. For example: a complainant's allegation was found not credible because she visited her alleged harasser at the hospital and at his brother's home and allowed him to come into her home alone at night after the alleged harassment occurred.[83] This information can be used as supportive evidence, but should not be used as determinative evidence alone to hold the allegations unfounded.

Any credible evidence that supports a witness' version of events can be corroborating evidence. For example, evidence from two independent witnesses that they personally heard the alleged harasser make certain statements towards the complainant can corroborate the complainant's story. Make a good faith effort to draw conclusions based on actual facts and not on some general observations or impressions.

2. Assessing Credibility

The issue of credibility is very important, particularly in sexual harassment cases where there are few eyewitnesses. The investigator should carefully review the credibility of both the complainant and the alleged harasser. A useful guide for determining the credibility of witnesses is found in the judgement of O'Halloran J. A, of British Columbia Court of Appeal in *Faryna v. Chorny:*[84]

Opportunities for knowledge, powers of observation, judgment and memory, ability to describe clearly what he has seen and heard, as well as other factors, combine to produce what is called credibility. ... The test must reasonably subject his story to an examination of its consistency with the probabilities that surround the currently existing conditions. In short, the real test of the truth of the story of a witness in such a case must be its harmony with the preponderance of the probabilities which a practical and informed person would readily recognize as reasonable in that place and in those conditions.

Unfortunately, an investigation often reveals two totally different accounts of the same events. Without eyewitnesses, the investigator is forced into deciding whom to believe. In determining credibility, consider the following factors (all are relevant, none are determinative):

(a) Checklist for Assessing Credibility

☑ Timing of the complaint. Was the complaint made contemporaneously with the incident or at a later date? If not contemporaneously, why not?

☑ What was the context in which the alleged harassment occurred?

☑ Were there any witnesses to the alleged harassment? Did the witnesses actually observe or hear anything?

☑ Were there opportunities that would permit the harassment to occur without being detected?

☑ Is there more than one person alleging harassment?

☑ Are there similar prior complaints in the alleged harasser's personnel file?

☑ Reputation - truthfulness of those involved.

☑ Motive - Did the complainant or other witnesses have any motive to lie? i.e., anger towards the alleged harasser, passed over for promotion, new assignment or transfer.

☑ Demeanour of all witnesses - Did the witness make eye contact? Be careful to consider the cultural background of the witness when evaluating the witness' demeanor. i.e., in some cultures, it may be considered rude to look another directly in the eye.

☑ Has the story been corroborated?

☑ Blanket denials without explanation?

☑ Were there inconsistencies which when confronted, the witness changed his/her original version of events?

3. Standard of Proof

It has frequently been asked: What is the "standard of proof" for sexual harassment complaints? In criminal cases the standard of proof is to prove the case *beyond a reasonable doubt*, whereas in civil cases the standard of proof as a rule is that of *on the balance of probabilities*. In harassment cases employers need not be sure beyond a reasonable doubt that an employee harassed a fellow worker.

Respondents generally argue that in sexual harassment cases the standard of proof should be somewhat higher than that of "on the balance of probabilities." They propose that the standard required to establish the complaint must be "clear and cogent" or "convincing." However, the Canadian courts and tribunals are overwhelmingly of the view that the standard of proof in human rights and sexual harassment complaints is that of on the balance of probabilities.

The B. C. Human Rights Tribunal in *Mahmoodi v. Dutton*[85] discussed at length the standard of proof for complaints of sexual harassment and concluded:

> ...the standard of proof for a complaint of sexual harassment is the balance of probabilities. The remedial purposes of human rights legislation do not trigger a lower standard. Similarly, the fact that the discrimination alleged is "sexual misconduct" by a professional does not elevate the standard of proof to a third standard which is closer to the criminal standard. Because a human rights proceeding is not the same as a professional or employment disciplinary proceeding, the principles with respect to the standard of proof, in those cases, are not necessarily directly analogous to this context. It is also unnecessary for a human rights tribunal to articulate a case specific test such as "clear and convincing" evidence.

On review, the B.C. Supreme Court[86] upheld the Tribunal's decision and confirmed that the standard of proof for sexual harassment complaints should be on the balance of probabilities.

As a rule of thumb, an employer faced with a sexual harassment complaint needs to conduct a **good-faith investigation** - one that is fair, objective and thorough then weigh the evidence and conclude what happened or probably happened. Looking at all the evidence and testimony, the investigator needs to determine whether or not the harassment occurred on the balance of probabilities (not beyond a reasonable doubt). The crux of an investigation may boil down to assessing the credibility of two witnesses with opposing testimony. In difficult cases, an investigator's findings may be inconclusive if he/she is unable to make a determination whether or not, the allegations are true even based on the less stringent standard of on the balance of probabilities.

4. Writing the Investigation Report

The investigation report should provide a complete record of what the investigator did or learned, including his/her findings. The report should state whether the allegations have been substantiated, unsubstantiated, found inconclusive, or whether the facts of the allegations were correct but the actions did not amount to sexual harassment.

The investigator should write his/her report in an even-handed manner. The tone of the report should be objective, neutral and non-argumentative. The investigator should be careful not to slant the evidence or give opinions. Let the facts on the record speak for themselves. Be careful not to use phrases such as "I think x", "I feel x", "I believe x", rather try to phrase the statement based on your observations: "Based on the evidence and the facts before me, I conclude that x."

Structure of the report:
The report may have the following sections:
(1) Introduction (or background);
(2) Summary (or Synopsis);
(3) Role and mandate of the investigator with reference to the policy;
(4) Investigative process - documents and evidence examined;
(5) Allegations made by the complainant;
(6) Responses to the allegations;
(7) Testimony of the interviewees - organized in groups;
(8) Findings; and
(9) Conclusions.
(See Appendix D - Sample Investigation Report Layout.)

H. Investigator's Checklist

Make sure that you have not overlooked anything.

Investigator's Checklist

☑ Review the employer's sexual harassment policy and procedures.

☑ Review applicable laws and statutes.

☑ Review the written complaint.

☑ Meet with the complainant.

☑ Meet with the alleged harasser?

☑ Review the personnel files of the complainant and the alleged harasser.

☑ What exactly was said and done - including physical details?

☑ What triggered the incident(s)?

☑ Is there any history of animosity between the parties involved?

☑ What is the personal and professional relationship between the parties?

☑ Whom did the complainant tell about the incident and when?

☑ How did the complainant and the alleged harasser react after the incident?

☑ Who are the witnesses to the incident?

☑ Interview all relevant witnesses.

☑ What were the witnesses' reactions?

☑ Keep detailed notes of interviews.

☑ Assess the credibility of witnesses.

☑ Don't be swayed by the emotions of the parties - maintain your objectivity.

☑ Review all documents, emails, and memorandums.

☑ Is there any physical evidence of the incident?

☑ Have you visited the location of the alleged harassment?

☑ Evaluate the evidence.

☑ Are other employees possibly being subjected to harassment from this alleged harasser?

☑ Were the complainant and alleged harasser aware of the employer's sexual harassment policy?

☑ Prepare the investigation report and present it to management.

CHAPTER 11

A. Communication of the Investigator's Findings

Once the investigation has been concluded, whether the allegations were substantiated, unsubstantiated, or found inconclusive, management should discuss the findings of the investigation with the complainant and the alleged harasser **in person**, separately, followed by a written notification. It should be management's function to inform the parties of the results of the investigation - the role of the investigator is only to provide the report of his/her findings to management.

There is some disagreement among the experts as to how much information about the investigation findings should be divulged to the complainant and the alleged harasser. Simply informing the parties that the investigation was concluded and whether or not the allegations were substantiated will not satisfy either party. On the other hand, to disclose the entire investigation report to the parties would involve supplying witnesses' names and statements and may breach confidentiality, privacy laws, and cause animosity among the workforce. Therefore, it may be advisable to give the complainant and the alleged harasser a synopsis or summary of the investigation findings that includes the reasons for the findings. In this way, confidentiality of the witnesses is protected and the alleged harasser and the complainant have sufficient information on which to decide if they wish to appeal or litigate.

1. Meeting with the Complainant

A management representative should meet with the complainant in person and explain that the company has completed its investigation. Advise the complainant of the results of the investigation and give the complainant a synopsis of the investigator's findings. The complainant should be given time to review and comment on the findings.

If the complaint was substantiated, the complainant will naturally be curious as to what measures are being taken to stop the harassment from continuing and what discipline, if any, the harasser received. This issue is somewhat controversial. Experts disagree as to how much information to divulge about the actions taken against the harasser. Some expert recommend revealing exactly what disciplinary measures were taken. For example, the harasser has been transferred, fired, financially penalized or warned. This information would satisfy the complainant's curiosity and would foster the feeling that the employer is serious about stopping harassment. However, the employer must be careful not to violate the harasser's privacy rights (under both federal and provincial laws) and not to defame him/her. On the other hand, some experts suggest simply telling the complainant that the matter has been resolved without providing any specifics about discipline or penalties imposed upon the harasser.

Probably the best course of action would be to balance the needs of satisfying the complainant's curiosity (and preventing rumors in the workplace) and preserving the harasser's privacy rights. Inform the complainant that steps have been taken to ensure that the behaviour does not happen again, and the harasser has been disciplined (if true) without providing any specifics of the type of discipline. [Note: The privacy laws are still developing in Canada, and the employer must ensure that it does not violate them.]

Assure the complainant that the employer will discuss appropriate remedies with her/him such as reinstatement, loss of wages, other benefits, compensation and apology, etc. Remind the complainant that the company has attempted to maintain confidentiality in every aspect of the investigation. Ask the complainant to inform any member of management or the sexual harassment advisor if there is any reoccurrence of the sexual harassment - or retaliation - from anyone.

Even if it was found that there was insufficient evidence to conclude that harassment occurred, a simple dismissal of the complaint is not sufficient. Give the complainant an opportunity to respond to the decision. It may be unpleasant, but be polite and sensitive. Make a note of the complainant's comments for the file. Also inform the complainant that he/she has the right to appeal under the company's harassment policy or to pursue the grievance procedure under the collective agreement, if any. Also advise the complainant that he/she has the right to file a complaint with the appropriate human rights commission.[87]

Thank the complainant for coming forward and filing a complaint. He/she should not hesitate to complain in the future if he/she feels harassed or retaliated against because of this complaint. You should also encourage the employee to come forward for any problems in the future.

2. Meeting with the Alleged Harasser

A management representative should meet with the alleged harasser in person and explain that the company has completed its investigation. Advise the alleged harasser of the results of the investigation and give the alleged harasser a synopsis of the investigator's findings. The alleged harasser should be given time to review and comment on the findings.

If the allegations have been proved and a decision has been made to discipline the harasser, another personal meeting should be arranged to inform the alleged harasser of the decision. Detailed notes of this meeting should be taken and placed both in the investigation file and in the alleged harasser's personnel file.

Begin the meeting by reviewing the allegations made in the sexual harassment complaint and then proceed to discuss how the investigation was conducted and the results of the investigation. The tone of the communication should be polite but firm. Do not make any derogatory remarks such as "You have been a harasser," etc. Do stress the company's disapproval of harassing behaviour (if found) and inform the alleged harasser that the behaviour was in violation of the company's sexual harassment policy.

Even if there was insufficient evidence to conclude that an incident of sexual harassment occurred, the alleged harasser should be advised of the company's sexual harassment policy and its commitment to a harassment free work environment. Remind the alleged harasser that retaliation is illegal and there should be no retaliation in any form against the complainant and/or other persons involved in the investigation. In certain situations (i.e., a malicious complaint), a letter of apology from the employer and/or the complainant to the alleged harasser may also be warranted.

B. Who Should Determine Penalty?

There is a difference of opinion among experts on whether the investigator should or should not suggest penalties and discipline. One view is that the investigator's function is simply to determine whether there is sufficient evidence to establish wrongdoing as alleged. Once it is found that sufficient evidence exists to support the allegations, the investigator's function is over. The investigator then sends his/her report to management. The investigator should not be involved in determining penalties, punishment, or discipline for the alleged harasser, and in determining remedies for the complainant. This function rests entirely in the hands of senior management.

Another view is that the investigator should suggest appropriate remedies - including the degree of discipline for the alleged harasser and the remedies for the victim. The function of actually imposing the discipline or awarding remedies still lies with management. Management may choose to accept the investigator's recommendations or change and modify them.

Most experts would agree that the investigator's objectivity (or at least perceived objectivity) is better maintained if he/she is not asked to recommend the remedy, including discipline of the alleged harasser. The division of function between the investigator and management is necessary to maintain the objectivity, neutrality and fairness of the investigation process. The function of determining discipline should lie with management, except in the case where the alleged harasser is a senior executive and the investigation is being conducted by an external investigator.

Let management face the consequences of its action or inaction. Management should accept this responsibility and impose discipline and penalty according to the company's policy of progressive discipline and past practices in view of the severity of the misconduct.

C. Disciplining the Alleged Harasser

The goal of the investigation, as stated earlier, is to determine if harassment did occur and if so, to effectively prevent it from happening again. The severity of the punishment depends on the nature and severity of the allegations, ranging from reprimand to termination.

Keep in mind that the punishment should mirror the offence. An unduly light penalty will send a wrong message - doing nothing is equal to sanctioning harassment in the workplace. One U.S. court held that an employer conducted an inadequate investigation because the employer did nothing. According to the employer, since the harassment did not occur again, there was nothing more it could do.

Discipline should be fair, reasonable, and uniform. It should be determined by assessing all of the circumstances, including:

- the seriousness of the harassing conduct;
- whether any of the company's guidelines or policies were violated;
- the alleged harasser's record of discipline, if any;

- the alleged harasser's conduct during the investigation, including demeanour, cooperation, willingness to accept responsibility, remorsefulness, willingness to apologize, and assurance for future good conduct;
- the alleged harasser's seniority with the company and performance history;
- the discipline imposed on other employees (at the same level) for committing a similar offense;
- whether there were any mitigating factors; and
- the company's goal and efforts to provide a harassment free environment.

Further, in a unionized workplace, discipline should also be in accordance with the collective agreement. In a non-unionized workplace, discipline should be administered uniformly in accordance with established practices.

D. False and Fabricated Accusations

Employers should encourage their employees to file a complaint if they feel they have been harassed. However, at the same time, employees should be aware that making false and fabricated accusations against innocent persons is a serious offence. A false and fabricated complaint is one in which the complainant knew or had reason to believe that the allegations made were untrue.

An individual may file a complaint for ulterior motives such as: animosity towards the alleged harasser,[88] to further her/his own ambition,[89] denial of a promotion, discipline or discharge for cause, breakdown of a romantic relationship, etc.

Employers should not allow complainants to make false and fabricated accusations with impunity. It has the potential to damage the reputation of the accused as well as that of the employer and can cause great stress and economic loss to both. Moreover, filing a false and fabricated complaint is a misuse of the dispute resolution process and undermines the employer's efforts to maintain a harassment free work environment.

If the investigation revealed that the complaint was frivolous, malicious, vexatious, or not made in good faith, the employer should let the complainant know that she/he may be subject to discipline. Human rights legislation is intended to protect employees from discrimination and harassment but not to shield those who make false accusations.

Employees should be aware that in addition to disciplinary action, a person making a false accusation might be subject to a defamation suit for slander under civil law. For example, a British Court awarded damages to a doctor falsely accused of sexual harassment by his female colleague in the amount of 150,000 pounds plus 100,000 pounds in costs.[90]

Of course, discipline would not be warranted in situations where the complainant filed the complaint in good faith, i.e., in circumstances where the complainant genuinely misconstrued the actions (or misinterpreted the words) of the alleged harasser; there was insufficient evidence; or because the conduct did not amount to harassment. The employer should ensure that the complainant is disciplined **only** for filing a false and fabricated complaint and not for being unable to substantiate the complaint.

Furthermore, some general warning to all employees would be in order either by staff meeting, memo, or company newsletter. Use this as an opportunity to educate the workforce - remind the employees of the company's policy and its commitment not to tolerate any kind of harassment and to provide a harassment free work environment.

E. Remedies for the Complainant

Once the investigation has established that sexual harassment did occur, employers have an obligation to provide adequate remedies for the complainant(s). Unlike courts and tribunals, an employer is not restricted by any legal doctrine or precedent in its choice to provide satisfactory redress for sexual harassment victims.

The nature and scope of remedies depends on the severity, frequency and duration of the harassment and its harmful effects on the complainant(s). The employer should attempt to undo the economic and job-related damage to the complainant, making the complainant *whole* again. That is, put the complainant in the position he/she would have been in *but for* the harassment. This may involve: reinstatement of lost wages or benefits; reinstating a lost opportunity or promotion; reimbursement for medical bills or counseling; and correcting personnel records.

The complainant may also require some job accommodations, such as a change in supervisor or duties. Always be sure to consult with the complainant regarding his/her wishes to avoid a retaliation charge before transferring the complainant to another position. Offer the complainant paid counseling if he/she requires it.

Employers often feel that disciplining the harasser is sufficient to resolve the complaint. However, that is not fair to the complainant nor will it avoid further litigation and liability. It should be pointed out that human rights tribunals have the power to award all sorts of monetary remedies. Complainants, if dissatisfied with the employer's response, have the right to file a complaint with the human rights commission. Once a complaint is filed with the commission, it becomes almost a public dispute.

Reinstatement

If the complainant was fired or constructively dismissed because of sexual harassment, the employer should reinstate or provide an equivalent job opportunity to the complainant **with back wages**.

Promotion

The complainant should be compensated for benefits that were lost due to the harassment. The employer should grant a promotion or bonus to the complainant if it was wrongfully denied.

Loss of Earnings

In cases where reinstatement is not viable, the employer should pay the complainant the wages he/she lost between the period when the complainant left the employment and when he/she acquired the next job.

1. Role of Apology

If the investigator is convinced that sexual harassment has occurred, management should promptly issue a written apology to the complainant. The employer should also ask the harasser to apologize to the victim. Though the employer cannot **force** the harasser to apologize, it can encourage him/her to do so.

 An apology for many complainants is very significant and healing. It sends a signal that the employer understands and acknowledges the problem. In addition to its therapeutic value for complainants, an apology allows the respondent to repent and to recognize his/her obligations under the *human rights laws*. If an apology is taken seriously, it is a step in the right direction. However, a true apology is a **voluntary** recognition by the respondent of having wronged another person.

Human rights tribunals used to grant the remedy of apology, but they have recently lost the authority to order employers to write a letter of apology to the victims of discrimination. In *Canada (Attorney General) v. Stevenson,*[91] the Tribunal had ordered the employer (Director of Canadian Security Intelligence Service) to issue a letter of apology for discrimination on the grounds of mental disability. A 2003 decision of the Federal Court set aside the order and stated that: "I cannot see how an apology under compulsion … can possibly serve to advance the primary focus of the *Canadian Human Rights Act*, which is eradication of discriminatory practices."[92]

An unwilling, grudgingly extracted apology does not indicate genuine remorse by the offender and therefore lacks the rehabilitation value for which an apology is sought. Although, tribunals no longer can award an apology as a remedy, employers are encouraged to issue a written apology because an apology still goes a long way towards healing the victim and restoring a positive atmosphere in the workplace.

F. When Harassment Was Not Found

In situations where the investigation did not substantiate the harassment complaint, or if the facts of the complaint were correct but the conduct did not amount to sexual harassment:

- ❖ The alleged harasser should be notified at once.
- ❖ The complainant should be encouraged to discuss his/her feelings (of frustration and anger) with a sympathetic co-worker, supervisor, or a counselor.
- ❖ In some situations, it would be beneficial to separate the complainant from the alleged harasser.
- ❖ The complainant should be informed that the employer's decision is not the last legal word on the matter - the complainant can still complain to the appropriate human rights commission. Additionally, the complainant could file a lawsuit for constructive dismissal (if the situation so warrants).

G. Monitor the Situation

Even prompt and strict disciplinary penalties for the harasser may not end the ordeal for the complainant. The harasser may continue his/her objectionable behaviour towards this complainant or towards others. There may be retaliation against the complainant by the alleged harasser, his/her friends and other co-workers who harbor grudges.

To guard against these possibilities, management should monitor the situation for an extended period of time. Hold follow-up meetings with the complainant to ensure that the harassment has ceased and that there has been no retaliation. Meet with the harasser on a regular basis to discuss his/her behaviour and provide any counseling or other help required. Keep a record of discussions with the harasser and the complainant.

H. Appeals and Complaints

As noted earlier, once the investigation is concluded, the investigator submits his/her report to management. If harassment is found, management then decides what penalties and discipline are to be imposed on the alleged harasser and what remedies are to be awarded to the complainant. Management then meets in person separately with the complainant and the alleged harasser to convey the findings of the investigator and the corrective actions. During this meeting, management should advise the complainant and the alleged harasser that they have a **right to appeal** under the organization's dispute resolution process, and the complainant also has a **right to file a complaint** with the appropriate human rights commission.

1. Appeal under the Policy

Even if you think that your organization has done an excellent job in handling the complaint, the complainant and the alleged harasser may disagree. Therefore, the employers should provide a mechanism for employees to appeal the findings of the investigator.

Right to Appeal

The company's sexual harassment policy should provide a right to appeal the findings of the investigation. The policy should outline such a procedure, including the terms, conditions, and time limits that are to be adhered to. A right to appeal the investigator's finding would foster greater confidence in the organization's policy and procedures and in its efforts to maintain a harassment free work environment. It would also improve the quality of the investigation because it is subject to review.

An appeal should be heard by a senior executive of the organization and preferably by an independent, outside neutral person. This person may be mentioned in the policy itself. An appeal procedure provides an opportunity for management to correct any errors that may have been committed during the investigation process. This would allow the organization to shield itself against embarrassment and adverse publicity that may result from an improper investigation.[93]

The purpose of the appeal process, however, is not to re-investigate a complaint. An appeal should be about the investigation process and/or the findings of the investigator, and not about the remedies awarded or the discipline imposed as a result of the investigator's findings. An appeal should relate to some specific concerns about the manner in which the investigation was handled, such as a critical piece of information was missed, a key witness was not interviewed, a crucial piece of evidence was not considered or the investigator was biased.

2. Complaint to the Commission

Employees have a statutory right to file a complaint with the appropriate human rights commission for any violation of the *Human Rights Act* - i.e., discrimination on prohibited grounds, including harassment and failure to provide a non-discriminatory work environment. Employees have the option to ignore the employer's complaint resolution process and file a complaint directly with the commission. It is, however, recommended that employees first file a complaint with the employer, and if they are dissatisfied by the remedial and corrective measures taken by management, only then file a complaint with the commission (watch for any statutory time limits).

As stated above, during the concluding session with the complainant, management should ensure that the complainant understands that he/she has the right to file a complaint with the commission (in B.C. directly with the Tribunal). It may be pointed out that efforts to discourage employees from filing a complaint with the commission or to retaliate for filing a complaint (or for assisting in filing a complaint) are illegal.

The commissions are administrative bodies established under the human rights statutes in each jurisdiction, and they are empowered to investigate and resolve complaints. The basic function of the commission is to investigate the complaint and determine whether the evidence warrants a hearing. The investigator's report may be submitted to the commission. The commission is not bound by the employer's investigation; however, a thorough, careful and timely investigation would have persuasive value.

The commission may dismiss the complaint or refer it to the tribunal for adjudication. A human rights tribunal is an adjudicative body, which hears and determines the matters referred to it by the commission. It acts like a civil court. Proceedings before the tribunal are public (i.e., any member of the public has the right to be present) and thus nothing remains confidential. Generally, the commission represents the public interest at these hearings. These hearings are usually lengthy and expensive.

The Tribunal either dismisses the complaint or upholds it and awards appropriate remedies including damages for loss of earnings and damages for loss of dignity and humiliation.

I. Remedial Action Checklist

After the conclusion of a sexual harassment investigation, the following checklist will be helpful to ensure that all appropriate actions were taken:

Remedial Action Checklist

☑ Investigator communicates the results of the investigation to management. Management should decide on the discipline, if any.

☑ Management communicates the results of the investigation by meeting separately in person with the complainant and the alleged harasser.

☑ Provide the alleged harasser and the complainant with a

synopsis of the investigation findings.

☑ Discipline should be appropriate to the gravity of harassment; and progressive discipline should be followed if the situation permits.

☑ Require the harasser to undergo counseling and sensitivity training (if necessary).

☑ Communicate to the complainant that the matter has been resolved and if the alleged harasser will be disciplined. Remember not to violate the alleged harasser's privacy rights.

☑ Discuss appropriate remedies ("make whole") with the complainant.

☑ Remind the harasser about no retaliation.

☑ Encourage the complainant to report any retaliation or further harassment from the alleged harasser or from others.

☑ Remind the harasser of the relevant provisions in the employer's sexual harassment policy (including zero tolerance).

☑ Ask the complainant whether he/she requires any job accommodations or counseling in light of all that has occurred.

☑ Point out to the complainant and to the alleged harasser that they have a right to appeal the investigator's findings under the organization's sexual harassment policy (if any).

☑ Point out to the complainant that she/he has an option to file a complaint with the human rights commission, if she/he is dissatisfied with the employer's decision.

☑ Monitor the situation to ensure further harassment is not occurring.

☑ Ensure the investigator maintains his/her investigation file with all the supporting documents received during and regarding the investigation in case of litigation or appeal.

☑ Follow up periodically with the complainant to check for further sexual harassment.

INVESTIGATION OF OTHER HUMAN RIGHTS COMPLAINTS

Although this text focuses on investigation of sexual harassment complaints, the principles, procedures and techniques described herein are equally applicable (with slight variances) to discrimination and harassment on all other prohibited grounds such as race, religion, age, national origin, marital status, sexual orientation and disability.

In some jurisdictions, statutes specifically prohibit harassment on the other grounds (for example, *Ontario Human Rights Code*). However, investigations of human rights complaints on the other prohibited grounds generally do not pose as complex and as delicate issues as sexual harassment complaints. Sexual harassment is usually an abuse of power where sexual favours are sought by threat or favour of job-related consequences; or where the work environment has become poisoned. Whereas harassment on the other prohibited grounds is mostly an expression of prejudice often systemic and built into the workplace culture.

Sexual harassment involves personal, emotional, and physical intimacy, and almost always occurs in a private setting where there are hardly any witnesses. Thus, it is problematic to ascertain whether the alleged sexual conduct was consensual or unwelcome and unwanted. It is usually not as difficult to ascertain whether the alleged harassment on the other prohibited grounds actually took place; rather the basic issue in harassment cases such as race, age or religion is to determine whether the employer knew about it and whether it did anything to stop it. A review of the general harassment cases indicate that in such cases, by and large, it is the employer's conduct (policy and procedures) that is under scrutiny, rather than the conduct of the individual harasser. Therefore, the number of investigations by employers into complaints of harassment on the other grounds compared to sexual harassment investigations are minimal.

Furthermore, harassment on the other discriminatory grounds has neither been the cause of a large number of complaints, nor of public or media attention to the same extent as sexual harassment. For example, in 2001, the Canadian Human Rights Commission received 167 harassment complaints, out of which 80% were sexual harassment complaints and only 20% were based on all other grounds combined. The issue of sexual harassment over the last few decades has been in the forefront of litigation, with American complainants settling or receiving court awards in the millions of dollars.

Nevertheless, employers and investigators can benefit from the investigative principles, techniques and methodologies described in this book for conducting investigations on all other prohibited grounds of discrimination and harassment.

APPENDICES

APPENDIX A

SAMPLE SEXUAL HARASSMENT POLICY

XYZ Company
Sexual Harassment Policy

Commitment

XYZ Company is proud of its tradition of maintaining a work environment in which all individuals are treated with respect and dignity. The company's policy is that all employees have the right to work in an environment free from discrimination and sexual harassment. Sexual harassment in the workplace is illegal and will not be tolerated. All employees, at all levels, must avoid offensive and inappropriate sexual and/or sexually harassing behaviour at work and in any situation related to employment. XYZ Company is committed to providing equality and impartiality in resolving complaints without fear and favour.

Scope

This policy applies to all employees, prospective employees, customers, clients, contractors, vendors and all others who do business with or are in contact with XYZ Company.

What is Sexual Harassment?

Sexual harassment includes offensive behaviour that is related to a person's sex as well as behaviour of a sexual nature that creates an intimidating, hostile or poisoned work environment. It also includes any behaviour that could reasonably be thought to put sexual conditions on a person's job or employment opportunities. Any sexually harassing conduct during work or work-related activities, whether physical, verbal or psychological committed by a supervisor, non-supervisory personnel, clients, customers or visitors is strictly prohibited. Such conduct may result in disciplinary action, including dismissal.

Examples of sexual harassment include, but are not limited to:

- unwelcome and unwanted sexual conduct;
- unwelcome sexual remarks, invitations or requests;
- displays of sexually explicit, sexist, or other offensive or derogatory material;
- written or verbal abuse or threats;
- jokes or practical jokes of a sexual nature;
- leering, staring, or other offensive gestures;
- unwelcome physical contact such as patting, touching, pinching, hitting;
- unwelcome advances, invitations, propositions of a sexual nature or repeated invitations after previous requests have been refused;
- any advances, invitations or propositions of a sexual nature which might, reasonably, be perceived as placing a condition on a person's employment, work assignment, or on any opportunity for training or promotion;
- requests for sexual favours;
- any verbal or physical conduct based on or related to sex that has the purpose or effect or creating an intimidating, hostile or offensive work environment;
- refusing to work with someone because of their sex or sexual orientation;
- remarks or innuendos about the sexual orientation

or personal life of a person; and
- sexual assault.

[Note: The harasser could be a man or a woman of either the same or opposite sex as the victim.]

What To Do If You Feel Sexually Harassed or Discriminated Against

Do not ignore it. Do not put up with it. Do something. Tell the instigator to STOP the behaviour. Sometimes a strong communication (whether verbal or in writing) that the behaviour is unwelcome is enough. For example: "I need to talk to you about the jokes you've been telling lately." "I find them sexist and offensive." "I would like you to stop telling them."

Note

If someone tells you that you did or said something that was inappropriate, offensive or harassing to them, don't immediately become defensive - listen - and try to see the situation from the other person's perspective. It may be that you have inadvertently been disrespectful, offensive or inadvertently harassed someone. This is a good time to correct the behaviour and apologize if necessary, before more serious measures are taken to stop the behaviour.

Informal Complaint:

If you don't feel comfortable approaching the instigator directly or if the behaviour does not stop, then report the matter to the sexual harasser advisor [Name], your supervisor, or the human resources manager. The sexual harassment advisor, supervisor or manager will inquire into the matter and try to resolve it. Document the events as completely as you can, including witnesses, dates, times, locations as this information will be necessary in case you file a formal complaint later.

Formal Complaint:

If the harassment did not cease by the harasser being told to stop the behaviour, or by other informal measures, or if you feel that the matter needs further attention, **file a formal complaint**. You can obtain a complaint form from _____. Be assured that XYZ Company will treat your complaint promptly, fairly, seriously and confidentially. Your complaint will be investigated by a qualified individual from inside or outside of the company. You will need to provide information about the harassment such as name of the alleged harasser(s); details of what happened; dates; times; places; how often the behaviour occurred; and witnesses' names. You will be kept informed about the progress of your complaint, and you will be informed of the investigation findings.

Complaints Against Senior Management

See Appendix B - Sample Policy Provisions Regarding Sexual Harassment Complaints Against Senior Management.

Retaliation Prohibited

All employees have the right to make a complaint or enforce their rights under this policy without fear of retaliation. Retaliation can be any adversely affected term of employment or discrimination against an employee who exercises his/her rights under the policy or the *Human Rights Act* and who files a complaint or assists in the investigation of a complaint. A person who retaliates will be treated in the same manner as a person who has harassed and will be subject to discipline. Examples of retaliation include:

- undue criticism of the complainant's work performance;
- failure to give promotion or work opportunities to the complainant;
- changing the complainant's job assignment;
- isolating or ridiculing the complainant; and
- discharge.

Complaints of such retaliation will be promptly investigated.

False Accusations

XYZ Company encourages victims of harassment to come forward and file complaints. However, at the same time, it should be pointed out that making false and a fabricated accusation against innocent persons is a serious offense. After investigation, if it is found that the complaint was frivolous, vexatious or not made in good faith, the complainant may be subject to discipline.

Mediation

XYZ Company encourages its employees to resolve disputes through mediation. Therefore the company offers mediation services to the parties if they so choose. The company will bear all the costs of the mediation including paid time-off for its employees. If the parties choose not to avail themselves of the mediation process then an investigation will take place.

Investigation

An investigator (whether internal or external) will be appointed to investigate your complaint. He/she will conduct a thorough and full investigation following the principles of natural justice and due process and will allow the parties full opportunity to present their case. The investigator will determine whether or not harassment occurred and he/she will provide a written report of the investigation's findings to [Name of Executive in the Organization] who will determine necessary corrective actions and penalties.

The complainant and respondent will be given _____days to review and comment on the investigator's findings. Comments are to be sent to the Vice-President of Human Resources [or other designate individual].

Corrective Action

If the investigation concludes that sexual harassment did occur, immediate and appropriate corrective and/or disciplinary action shall be taken. Corrective measures, proportionate to the seriousness of the offense, may range anywhere from a verbal or written warning to suspension, transfer, and even dismissal for an harasser. Appropriate remedies will be provided to the victim if so warranted.

Appeals

If dissatisfied with the investigation's findings, the complainant and/or the alleged harasser have the right to file an appeal with [Title and Name of Executive in the Organization] within _____ days of hearing the determination of the investigation. If the executive member mentioned above, believes that there are sufficient grounds to conduct further investigation, he/she may do so.

Consensual Relationships

XYZ Company particularly warns supervisors against engaging in sexual or romantic relationships with a subordinate. Due to the fact that it is very difficult to prove that such relationships are consensual, the company is vulnerable to sexual harassment claims. Therefore, supervisors should be aware that the company regards consensual relationships between supervisors and subordinates as inappropriate. In the event that a consensual relationship does develop between a supervisor and a subordinate, the sexual harassment advisor should be notified immediately so that appropriate measures may be taken to protect all parties involved.

Confidentiality

All persons involved with the investigation of a complaint, including the complainant and the respondent, are required to maintain confidentiality except where disclosure is necessary for the purposes of investigating the matter, imposing a penalty contemplated by this policy, or as required by law. XYZ Company will make every effort to ensure the confidentiality of the complainant and the alleged harasser to the degree permitted by law.

Other Avenues of Redress

This procedure does not deny or limit access to other avenues of redress available under the law [i.e., criminal complaint, civil suit, grievance or a complaint with the appropriate human rights commission]. The investigator may decide to postpone, suspend or cancel the investigation should any of these avenues be pursued.

Time Limits

Complaints should be filed as quickly as possible, but not later than ____ months from the time of the alleged incident.

Policy Distribution

All new employees shall be given a copy of this policy upon commencement of employment. Updates will also be distributed from time to time. Complaint reporting procedures and other pertinent information shall be posted on [Name and Location] bulletin boards and on the company website at: [website address].

XYZ Company will review this policy periodically and will make adjustments where necessary. If you have any concerns or comments about this policy please bring them to the attention of [Human Resources Representative]. XYZ Company is committed to a harassment free work environment and will do all that it can to achieve it.

[**Note**: These sample provisions may be adapted to conform to your organization's needs. You should consult your lawyer to ensure that these provisions are appropriately modified to conform to your organization's size, structure, policies and other requirements of your particular organization, and privacy and other applicable laws.]

APPENDIX B

SAMPLE POLICY PROVISIONS FOR COMPLAINTS AGAINST SENIOR MANAGEMENT

[Note : These provisions can be incorporated into the company's sexual harassment policy or preferably, the company can form a separate sexual harassment policy for senior management.]

<u>XYZ Company</u>
<u>Sexual Harassment Policy For Complaints</u>
<u>Against Senior Management</u>

Commitment

XYZ Company is committed to providing equality and impartiality in resolving complaints against senior management without fear and favour. These complaints will be handled by a qualified External Consultant.

External Consultant

Complaints regarding the "direct personal behaviour" of members of the Board of Directors, the Chief Executive Officer, the Chief Financial Officer, General Manager, the Director of Human Resources, or any senior executive will be handled by an External Consultant. You can obtain the name and contact information for the External Consultant by visiting our website at: [website address], or posted on the bulletin board located at _____ . The External Consultant is not an employee of XYZ Company and will maintain your complaint in confidence to the maximum degree permitted by law.

Filing of the Complaint

An employee who feels that he/she has been sexually harassed by a senior executive (described above) should file a complaint directly with the External Consultant as named above.

Notification of Complaint

The Consultant shall notify the secretary of the Board of Directors (or the Executive Committee) of all complaints immediately upon receipt. The Consultant shall notify the persons named in the complaint of the specific allegations against them as soon as possible thereafter.

Power and Functions of the Consultant

The Consultant has the power to investigate and/or attempt to settle the complaint, and to speak with anyone, examine any documents and enter any work location relevant to the complaint for the purposes of investigation or settlement.

Investigation

The Consultant will conduct a thorough and full investigation following the principles of natural justice and due process and allow the parties full opportunity to present their case.

Interim Reports and Discontinuance of Complaint

The Consultant may make interim reports to the Board of Directors (or the Executive Committee), as required, to address instances of interference, obstruction, retaliation, or breaches of confidentiality encountered by the Consultant while dealing with a complaint under this policy.

Upon receipt of the complaint, or at any point during the investigation/mediation, the Consultant may submit a report to the Board of Directors recommending that the Board discontinue dealing with a complaint where an adequate remedy already exists; the complaint is frivolous, vexatious or not made in good faith; or, having regard to all the circumstances, further investigation of the matter is unnecessary.

The Board of Directors may approve or reject the recommendations after considering submissions from the parties to the complaint.

Consultant Final Report

The Board of Directors shall be presented with a final report outlining the findings, conclusions, recommended corrective actions, or terms of settlement, within_____days of the making of the complaint. The Board of Directors may grant an extension of time upon the request of the Consultant.

The complainant and respondent will be given _____days to review and comment on the investigator's findings. Comments are to be sent to the Board of Directors.

Final Decision

The Board of Directors will review the final report and any comments received from the parties before making any decision on the matter. The Board may approve, change or reject any proposed terms of settlement or recommended corrective action.

The Consultant will be responsible for monitoring the implementation of the Board's decision and for providing regular progress reports to the Board.

Confidentiality

All persons involved with a complaint, including the complainant and respondent, are to maintain confidentiality except where disclosure is necessary for the purposes of investigating the matter or as required by law.

Other Avenues of Redress

This procedure does not deny or limit access to other avenues of redress available under the law [i.e., criminal complaint, civil suit, or a complaint with the appropriate human rights commission]. The Consultant may decide to postpone, suspend or cancel any process underway should any of these avenues be pursued.

Time Limits

The time limit for the filing of complaints is ___ months from the time of the alleged incident of harassment.

[**Note**: These sample provisions may be adapted to conform to your organization's need. You should consult your lawyer to ensure that these provisions are appropriately modified to conform to your organization's size, structure, policies and other requirements of your particular organization, and privacy and other applicable laws.]

APPENDIX C

SAMPLE SEXUAL HARASSMENT COMPLAINT FORM

<u>XYZ Company</u>
<u>Sexual Harassment Complaint Form</u>

PART I

Complainant's Name: _____

Address: _____

Telephone Number: _____

Department: _____

Position/Job Title: _____

Name of Immediate Supervisor: _____

PART II

Describe the nature of harassment:

_____

_____

_____

_____

Person who was responsible for the harassment:

Name: _____

Position: _____

Supervisor: ❑   Co-worker: ❑

Customer/Client: ❑   Other: ❑

Date and Time of the Incident:

_____

Did it occur more than once? Yes ❑ No ❑
   • Did it occur during your working hours?
   • When did it start?
   • When did it stop?
   • Is it still going on?

Location of Incident:
   • Was it at the workplace?
   • Was it off of the premises?
Describe the circumstances in which the incident took place:

_____

_____

_____

_____

What was your reaction?   _____

   How did you feel?   _____

Did you do anything or talk to anyone after the incident?

   Give details: _____

_____

_____

_____

_____

_____

PART III

Describe the incident: _____

_____

_____

Was it the first and only incident? _____

       If not, list all previous incidents including time, place and nature of the events: _____

_____

_____

_____

List Witnesses to the harassment:

(1) Name: _____

    Department: _____

    Home Phone: _____

(2) Name: _____

    Department: _____

    Home Phone: _____

I understand that the incident(s) described above will be investigated, I will be given an opportunity to explain further, and I will be informed of the results of the investigation.

Complainant's Signature_____

Date:_____

FOR OFFICE USE ONLY

Matter was referred to investigation on _____ date.

Investigation was completed on _____ date.

Final Report was produced on _____ date.

Complaint was: established / not established

Parties were informed of outcome on _____ date.

Action taken: _____

_____

_____

[**Note:** Make the complaint form part of your sexual harassment policy. Consult with your lawyer to ensure that the complaint form is suitable to your organizational needs and meets with the legal requirements of your province or state.]

APPENDIX D

SAMPLE INVESTIGATOR'S REPORT LAYOUT

<u>XYZ Company</u>
<u>Investigation Report</u>

Name of Investigator: _____

Date investigation began: _____

Date investigation was concluded: _____

Name of the Complainant: _____

Name of the Alleged Harasser: _____

Nature of the Allegations: _____

    ❏ Complaint was substantiated

    ❏ Complaint was unsubstantiated

    ❏ Findings were inconclusive

    ❏ Conduct did not amount to sexual harassment

Introduction

_____

_____

_____

_____

Synopsis of Findings

_____

_____

Scope of the Investigation (role and mandate of the investigator)

_____

_____

_____

Summary of Interviews

_____

_____

_____

_____

Documents Reviewed

_____

_____

_____

Findings

_____

_____

_____

Conclusions

_____

_____

_____

Signature of the Investigator:_____

Date Report Submitted:_____

ENDNOTES

[1] *Olarte v. Commodore Business Machines Ltd.* (0nt. 1983), 4 C.H.R.R. D/1705 (Cumming) at 1734; affd (sub nom. *Commodore Business Machines Ltd. v. Ont. Minster of Labour*) (Ont. 1985), 6 C.H.R.R. D/2833 (Div. Ct.).

[2] See *S.E.P.Q.A. v. Canada*, (C.H.R.C.) [1989] 2 S.C.R. 879 at 898; 62 D.L.R. (4th) 385 (S.C.C.).

[3] *Bell v. Ladas*, (Ont. 1980), 1 C.H.R.R. D/155 (Shime).

[4] *Ibid.*

[5] *Janzen v. Platy Enterprises Ltd.*, (Man. 1989), 10 C.H.R.R. D/6205 (S.C.C.).

[6] *Ibid.* at D/6227 (para. 44451).

[7] *Olarte v. Commodore Business Machines Ltd.*, *supra note* 1.

[8] *Janzen v. Platy Enterprises Ltd.*, *supra* note 5.

[9] For further analysis of same-sex sexual harassment *see:* Arjun P. Aggarwal & Madhu M. Gupta, *Sexual Harassment in the Workplace* and *Same-Sex Sexual Harassment: Is it Sex Discrimination? A Review of Canadian and American Law*, Manitoba Law Journal Vol. 27 No. 3 (2001).

[10] *Romman v. Sea-West Holdings Ltd.*, (Can. 1984) 5 C.H.R.R. D/2312 (Jones).

[11] *Cassidy v. Sanchez*, (B.C. 1988), 9 C.H.R.R. D/5278, (Wilson).

[12] *Van Berkel v. MPI Security Ltd.*, (B.C. 1996) 28 C.H.R.R. D/504 (Attafuah).

[13] *Hanes v. M&M Ventures and Wight*, (Sask. 1998), 99 CLLC, Para. 230-001.

[14] *Kavanagh v. Canada (Attorney General)* (2001), 41 C.H.R.R. D/119 (C.H.R.T.).

[15] *Montreuil v. National Bank of Canada*, (Feb. 2004) (C.H.R.T.) (unreported).

[16] *Robichaud v. Canada*, (1987) 40 D.L.R. (4th) 577 (S.C.C.); (Can. 1987) 8 C.H.R.R. D/4326 (S.C.C.).

[17] *Thessaloniki Holdings Ltd. v. Saskatchewan Human Rights Commission*, (Sask. 1991), 91 CLLC para. 17,029 (Q.B.).

[18] *EEOC v. Sage Realty Corporation* 507 F.Supp. 599 (SDNY 1981).

[19] See *Woiden, Falk, Yeary & Curle v. Dan Lynn* (Can. 2002) 43 C.H.R.R. D/296 (Hadjis).

[20] See *Ferguson v. Muench Works Ltd.*, (B.C. 1997) 33 C.H.R.R. D/87 (Williamson).

[21] *Robichaud v. Canada supra note 16.*

[22] *Robichaud v. Canada supra note 16.*

[23] *Robichaud v. Canada supra note* 16 at D/4334 (Para 33946).

[24] *Fleet Industries v. Int'l Ass'n of Machinists and Aerospace Workers*, (1997) unreported (Picher).

[25] *Ibid.*

[26] *Ferguson v. Muench, supra note 20.*

[27] *Faragher v. City of Boca Raton*, 118 S.Ct. 2275 (1998).

[28] *Burlington Industries Inc. v. Ellerth*, 118 S. Ct. 2257 (1998).

[29] *Fall* v. *University of Indiana*, 12 Supp. 2d. 870 (N.D. Ind. 1998).

[30] *Drummond v. Tempo Paint & Varnish Co.*, (Ont. 1998) 33 C.H.R.R. D/175 (Laird).

[31] *Wilgan v. Wendy's Restaurants of Canada Inc.*, (B.C. 1990) 11 C.H.R.R. D/119 (Barr).

[32] See *Karlenzigg v. Chris Holdings Ltd.*, (Sask. 1991) 15 C.H.R.R. D/5 (Rooney). *See also Uzoaba v. Correctional Services*, (Can. 1994) (unreported) (Mactavish) application for judicial review denied April 20, 1998.

[33] See *McMorrow & Treasury Bd.* 166-2-2390 and *Seneca College v. OPSEU* [1996] 57 LAC (4th) 343 (Keller), the Board held that as the employer did not follow its own policy and failed to bring the matter against the grievor as alleged, the Board refused to uphold her discharge.

[34] *See* for example, *OPSEU (HURGE) and Ontario Ministry of Attorney General*, (1995) GSB 348/92, (unreported) (Kaplan).

[35] *Okanagan University College* and *Okanagan University College Faculty Assn.*, (1997) 64 L.A.C. 4th, 416 (Lanyon).

[36] For further analysis *see* "Sexual Harassment in the Unexpected" in the author's text, Arjun P. Aggarwal & Madhu M. Gupta, *Sexual Harassment in the Workplace* 65-100 (Butterworths 3rd ed. 2000).

[37] *See* "Favours for Submission" discussed in the author's text, *Sexual Harassment in the Workplace, ibid.* at 171.

[38] *See Sexual Harassment in the Workplace, supra* note 36 at 453.

[39] *See Masters v. Ontario,* (1994), 18 O.R. (3rd) 551 (Div. Ct.).

[40] *Ibid.*

[41] *See Van Zamt v. KLM Royal Dutch Airlines,* 80 F.3d. 708-715 (2nd Cir. 1996).

[42] *See Dovtz v. City of New York,* 904 F. Supp. 127, 154 (S.D.N.Y. 1995).

[43] *See Walsh v. National Westminister Bancorp,* 921 F. Supp. 168, 173 (S.D.N.Y. 1995).

[44] *Saxton v. AT&T,* 10 F. 3d 526, 535 (7th Cir 1993). S*ee also Nash v. Electrospace Systems, Inc.* 9 F.3d 401, 404 (5th Cir. 1993) where the prompt investigation was completed within one week and *Juarez v. Ameritech Mobile Communications, Inc.,* 957 F. 2d 317, 319 (7th Cir. 1992) where the investigation was completed within four days.

[45] *See Masters v. Ontario, supra note* 39.

[46] *See Slattery v. Canadian Human Rights Commission,* (1994) 2 F.C. 574 (T.D.) and *Miller v. Canada,* (1996), 12 F.T.R. 195.

[47] *See Masters v. Ontario, supra note* 39.

[48] *See Grover v. National Research Council,* (2001) F.C.T. June 21, 2001.

[49] *Ibid.*

[50] *See Singh v. Canada (Attorney General),* (2001) F.C.J. No. 367.

[51] *See Charleston v. Canada,* (1998) F.C.A. #1353 (F.C.T.D.).

[52] *Ruckpaul v. Canada (Ministry of Citizenship and Immigration),* Jan. 30, 2004 (unreported) (File No. T-31-02).

[53] *OPSEU v. Ministry of Attorney General,* (1995) G.S.B. No. 348/92 (unreported) (Kaplan).

54 *McIntyre v. Rogers Cable T.V. Ltd.*, (1996) B.C. J. No. 200.

55 *Canada (Information Commissioner) v. Canada (Minister of Citizenship)* 2002 F.C.A. 270, (paras. 34, 35, 37 and 38).

56 *School District No. 33 v. Chilliwack Teachers' Association*, (B.C. 1990), 16 L.A.C. (4th) 94 (Hope).

57 *McIntyre v. Rogers Cable T.V. Ltd., supra note* 54.

58 *Shiels v. Saskatchewan Government Insurance*, (1988), 51 D.L.R. (4th) 28 (Sask. Q.B.).

59 *Hewes v. City of Etobicoke*, (1991), 92 C.L.L.C. 14, 001 (Ont. Gen. Div.). In this case, Mr. Hewes, a utilities superintendent of 38 years seniority, was dismissed for allegedly sexually harassing (fondling of breasts) a female radio clerk in his office just three years prior to his retirement.

60 *MacLean v. Treasury Board*, (1993), PSSRB File No. 166-2-22580 (Tenace).

61 *Gravel v. Canada (Treasury Board)*,(1991), PSSRB File No. 166-2-21603 (PSSRB).

62 *Samra v. Treasury Board (Indian and Northern Affairs)*, (1996) PSSRB File No. 166-2-26543 (Tenace).

63 *Yeomans v. Simon Fraser University*, (1996) B.C. J. No. 956.

64 Public Policy Sources 25, by David Finlay, The Fraser Institute, contains extensive analysis of handling sexual harassment complaints and the university's sexual harassment policy.

65 *Leach v. Canadian Blood Services,* [2001] A.J. No. 119.

66 *MacLean v. Treasury Board, supra note* 60.

67 *Slattery v. Canadian Human Rights Commission, supra note* 46.

68 *Miller v. Canada, supra note* 46.

69 *Charleston v. Canada, supra note* 51.

70 *Grover v. National Research Council, supra note* 48.

71 *Singh v. Canada (Attorney General), supra note* 50.

[72] *Ruckpaul v. Canada (Ministry of Citizenship and Immigration), supra note* 52.

[73] *See Wilgan v. Wendy's Restaurants of Canada Inc., supra note* 31.

[74] *Springsteel v. Brick Warehouse Corp.*, [2003] A.J. No. 1402 (Alt. Ct. of Queen's Bench).

[75] *See Gower v. Tolko Manitoba*, (2001), 153 Man. Rep. (2nd) 20, (C.A.).

[76] *See Miller v. CHRC*, (1996) 112 F.T.R. 185, (Para. 18).

[77] *See OPSEU v. Ontario Ministry of Attorney General*, (Hurge grievance) (April 24, 1995) (unreported) (Kaplan).

[78] Professor Shirley Ketz of York University uses and recommends the use of a note-taker: *see How to do an Investigation*, a supplement to CAPDHEE Newsletter (2001).

[79] *See Gravel v. Canada (Treasury Board), supra note* 61 and *MacLean v. Treasury Board, supra note* 60.

[80] *See for example Canada (Information Commissioner) v. Canada (Ministry of Citizenship), supra note* 55.

[81] *McIntyre v. Rogers Cable T.V. Ltd., supra note* 54.

[82] *McIntyre v. Rogers Cable T.V. Ltd., supra note* 54.

[83] *Sardigal v. St. Louis Nat'l Stockyards Company*, 42 Fair Empl. Prac. Cas. (BNA) (S. D. Ill. 1986).

[84] *Faryna* v. *Chorny*, [1952] 2 D. L. R. 354 at 356-58 (B.C. C. A.).

[85] *Mahmoodi v. Dutton*, (1999) 36 C.H.H.R. D/8 at D/23 (para. 148 to 151) (B.C. Tri.).

[86] *Dutton v. British Columbia (Human Rights Tribunal)*, (2001) 41 C.H.R.R. D/10 (B.C. S.C.).

[87] *See* discussion infra under Appeals and Complaints.

[88] *See* for example, *Hewes v. City of Etobicoke, supra note* 59.

[89] *See* for example, *McIntyre v. Rogers Cable T.V. Ltd., supra note* 54.

90 *See* 11 The Lawyers Weekly, No.30, p.20 (December 6, 1991).

91 *Canada (Attorney General) v. Stevenson,* 2003 F.C.T. 341 (unreported).

92 *Ibid.* at para. 33.

93 For example, *see* David Finlay "The Trial of Liam Donnelly – Conviction by Prejudice," Public Policy Sources 25, The Fraser Institute 1999. In this case if the university had an appeal procedure, perhaps it would have corrected the unfairness of the investigation and thus avoided the humiliation and adverse publicity.